55
ANSWERS
TO QUESTIONS ABOUT
LIFE AFTER
DEATH

MARK HITCHCOCK

55
ANSWERS

TO QUESTIONS ABOUT

LIFE AFTER
DEATH

Multnomah® Publishers *Sisters, Oregon*

55 ANSWERS TO QUESTIONS ABOUT LIFE AFTER DEATH
published by Multnomah Publishers, Inc.
© 2005 by Mark Hitchcock
International Standard Book Number: 1-59052-436-5
Cover design by The DesignWorks Group, Inc.
Interior design and typeset by Katherine Lloyd, The DESK

Italics in Scripture are the author's emphasis.
Unless otherwise indicated, Scripture quotations are from: New American Standard
Bible® © 1960, 1977, 1995 by the Lockman Foundation. Used by permission.

Other Scripture quotations are from:
Holy Bible, New Living Translation (NLT) © 1996.
Used by permission of Tyndale House Publishers, Inc. All rights reserved.
The Oxford Annotated Apocrypha, expanded edition.
Revised Standard Version, 1977. Used by permission.
The Holy Bible, New International Version (NIV) © 1973, 1984 by International
Bible Society, used by permission of Zondervan Publishing House
The Holy Bible, King James Version (KJV)
The Message © 1993 by Eugene H. Peterson
The New English Translation (NET) © 1996–2003 Biblical Studies Press
Scripture quoted by permission. Quotations designated NET are
from The Holy Bible: The NET Bible® (New English Translation®).
www.netbible.com. All rights reserved.

Multnomah is a trademark of Multnomah Publishers, Inc.,
and is registered in the U.S. Patent and Trademark Office.
The colophon is a trademark of Multnomah Publishers, Inc.

Printed in the United States of America

For information:
MULTNOMAH PUBLISHERS, INC.
POST OFFICE BOX 1720 • SISTERS, OREGON 97759

Library of Congress Cataloging-in-Publication Data

Hitchcock, Mark.
  55 answers to questions about life after death / Mark Hitchcock.
    p. cm.
Includes bibliographical references (p. 247).
ISBN 1-59052-436-5
  1. Future life--Christianity. I. Title: Fifty five answers to questions about life after
death. II. Title.
  BT903.H58 2005
  236'.2--dc22   2004022959

05 06 07 08 09 10 11—10 9 8 7 6 5 4 3 2 1

To Bruce DeFriese

*Thank you for your faithful friendship
and godly example to me and my family.
I will always treasure our times
of fellowship in the Word together.
You are "my brother and fellow worker
and fellow soldier" (Philippians 2:25).*

Contents

Introduction

> To die would be an awfully big adventure.
>
> PETER PAN

If a man dies, will he live again?"
Four thousand years ago, in the wake of deep personal tragedy, suffering, and death, a man named Job asked the question of the ages (Job 14:14). Since the dawn of history, the subject of death and the afterlife has been the great question of human existence.

Not long ago the Discovery Channel featured a program about the ten great mysteries of the world. The mysteries included the lost city of Atlantis, UFOs, Bigfoot, Stonehenge, and the Loch Ness Monster. But the overwhelming number one mystery was life after death. It's a subject that everyone wonders about. What lies behind the veil of death? Is there really life after our final breath? Is there a place called hell? Does purgatory actually exist? Is heaven a real place? Who will be in heaven?

More Americans than ever—81 percent—now say that they believe in life after death. Since the turn of the century, belief in an afterlife among American Catholics, Jews, and those with no religious affiliation has grown significantly. Even so, as more people profess to believe in life after death, it seems that most don't have much of an idea about what happens to people when they die. Questions abound. Inquiring minds want to know.

In this answer-packed, fast-paced book I want to clearly and simply address the real questions that people like you and me have about what awaits us beyond the grave.

The Bible doesn't answer all the questions we have about the afterlife, but I think you'll be amazed at how much the pages of Scripture do reveal about this intriguing topic.

Join me as we take a sneak peek behind the curtain of death, as we see what the Bible says about death and the reality of life after life.

My prayer is that God will use this book to help us live more faithfully for Christ in this life…and long more fully to be with Him in the next.

—*Mark Hitchcock*
Faith Bible Church
Edmond, Oklahoma

PART ONE

Unlocking Life's Greatest Mystery

Chapter 1

WHAT IS DEATH?

Before we can understand life after death, we must first get a handle on what death means. What does the Bible tell us about death? What are some of the key truths about death that we need to understand?

Here's a big one right off the top: *The Bible teaches us that death comes quickly.* I heard a story recently about a man who went to the doctor. The conversation went like this.

"I'm afraid I have bad news, Mr. Smith," said the doctor. "You don't have long to live."

"Really?" said the patient. "How long?"

"Ten," said the doctor.

"Ten?" asked the patient. "TEN! Ten *what?* Ten months? Ten weeks? *What?*"

The doctor responded, "Nine, eight, seven, six…"[1]

One of the truths the Bible emphasizes again and again is the brevity of human life. Every picture of human life in the pages of Scripture stresses its ephemeral nature.

The duration of human life is pictured as a flower that

blooms in the morning and withers in the afternoon sun, a shadow that appears and fades away, a morning mist or fog that dissipates with the rising sun (Job 14:2; Psalm 90:5–6).

A Sharper Image catalog a few years ago advertised a "Personal Life Clock." In a crisp, full-color image, the catalog displayed a marble obelisk with digital numbers that flashed the number of hours, minutes, and seconds remaining in one's "statistical life-time." The sales copy noted, "All lives are finite. In fact, the average life lasts only 683,280 hours, or 2.4 billion seconds. This new Timisis Personal Life Clock reminds you to live life to the fullest by displaying the…most profound number you will ever see."

A few years ago, when Billy Graham was in his early eighties, an interviewer asked him what had surprised him most about life. Without hesitation, Dr. Graham replied, "Its brevity." The older we get, the faster the sands of time seem to leak through the glass. One important thing the Bible and experience teach us about death is that it comes quickly.

Here's another central biblical truth about death: *It's not the end.* I once heard a story about an ancient king who called a group of scholars to his palace to write a history of mankind. As they labored through the years, the scholars compiled numerous volumes. The king, however, was always too busy to read them. When the king was very old, he again called the scholars to the palace and asked them to give him a summary of their findings. The leader of the group said, "Man was born, he suffered, he died. That is the history of mankind."

There's a lot of truth in that summary.

But it's not complete.

What about *after* "he died"? Death is not the end of man's history. Death in the Bible always means separation, never annihilation or cessation of existence.

In the Garden of Eden, remember, God told Adam that the day he ate of the fruit of the tree of the knowledge of good and evil he would surely die (Genesis 2:17). When our first parents disobeyed that command, they did not immediately fall over dead. But in that moment, they *began* to die physically. Adam died 930 years later. But the very instant they ate the fruit, they died spiritually, just as God had said. They found themselves separated and alienated from God. Adam and Eve sensed their guilt and shame before God and made garments out of leaves to cover their naked bodies and hide their sin.

A person who is *spiritually dead* is a person who is spiritually separated from God (Ephesians 2:1). Likewise, when a person dies *physically*, he or she does not cease to exist. There is a separation between the material part (body) and immaterial part (soul/spirit) of the person. When this separation occurs, the body "falls asleep" and is buried. But the soul, the immaterial part of the person, goes to one of two places.

In the Bible there are three different aspects to death. But in each case the key idea is separation, not cessation.

First, there is spiritual death—the separation of sinful man from a holy Creator. Fallen man is "dead in [his] trespasses and sins" (Ephesians 2:1). "But your iniquities have made a separation between you and your God, and your sins have hidden His face from you, so that He does not hear" (Isaiah 59:2). This separation was bridged for us by Jesus when He died on the cross and bore the penalty for our sins in His body. By the grace of God, Jesus tasted death for every person (Hebrews 2:9).

Second, there is physical death—the separation of the temporary, material body from the eternal, immaterial part of man when life on earth ends. The Bible says that "the body without the spirit is dead" (James 2:26). The opposite, however, is never true. The immaterial part of man was created to live forever.

When he was created, Adam was just an empty "clay pot" made from the dust of the earth. Then the Lord God "breathed into his nostrils the breath of life; and man became a living being" (Genesis 2:7). Adam was not a person—he had no life—until he had a soul. Your soul is the real you. It's what gives eternal value to your being. So when you die, life does not—cannot—end because your soul is eternal.

Physical death, then, is not a period; it's a *conjunction*. The world often puts a period after death, but God puts a conjunction. Notice in Luke 16:22 that when Lazarus died, it says, "the poor man died *and.*" Then when the rich man died, again it says, "the rich man also died *and.*" The story Jesus told in Luke 16 could have been very brief if Jesus had simply said, "The poor man died, and the rich man died. Period." That would have been the abrupt end to the story.[2] But physical death is not cessation. At the split second we die, our spirit passes into conscious existence in eternity.

Third, there is eternal death—the eternal separation of lost sinners in hell from the presence of God. "These will pay the penalty of eternal destruction, away from the presence of the Lord and from the glory of His power" (2 Thessalonians 1:9). This final aspect of death is called the "second death" because it follows physical death (Revelation 20:6, 14). We will discover a lot more about the second death in part 3 of this book, beginning with question 14.

For now, let's turn to the next step. What happens after a person dies physically? Where does the soul go?

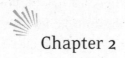

Chapter 2

WHERE DO PEOPLE GO WHEN THEY DIE?

Perhaps you've read about the weathered tombstone in an old cemetery in Indiana that bears this epitaph:

Pause, stranger, when you pass me by;
As you are now, so once was I,
As I am now, so you will be,
So prepare for death and follow me.

An unknown passerby read those words and etched this reply below them:

To follow you I'm not content,
Until I know which way you went.[3]

That passerby was right on. The most important thing to know about dying is "What follows death?" Or to be more specific, "Where are you going?"

As we have seen, the Bible teaches that physical death means separation. But separation to what—or where? Where does the departed spirit of man go?

The answer is very simple: to one of two eternal destinations.

Physical death brings immediate passage into the next life. I like what Tony Evans says: "Most people think we are in the land of the living on our way to the land of the dying, but actually, we are in the land of the dying on the way to the land of the living."[4]

In the fascinating parable of the rich man and Lazarus in Luke 16, Jesus pulls back the corner of the veil of death and gives us just a brief glimpse into the two destinations for all people: heaven and hell. We see in this story Jesus told that both Lazarus and the rich man ended up somewhere when they died. Death is followed by a destination.

The split second a person dies, his or her soul/spirit immediately goes to one of two places, depending solely on that individual's relationship with Jesus Christ.

The departed soul/spirit of a believer in Christ goes immediately into the presence of the Lord, while the body falls asleep.

> "Now there was a rich man, and he habitually dressed in purple and fine linen, joyously living in splendor every day. And a poor man named Lazarus was laid at his gate, covered with sores, and longing to be fed with the crumbs which were falling from the rich man's table; besides, even the dogs were coming and licking his sores. Now the poor man died and was carried away by the angels to Abraham's bosom; and the rich man also died and was buried." (Luke 16:19–22)

We are of good courage, I say, and prefer rather to be absent from the body and to be at home with the Lord. (2 Corinthians 5:8)

For to me, to live is Christ and to die is gain. But I am hard-pressed from both directions, having the desire to depart and be with Christ, for that is very much better. (Philippians 1:21, 23)

A grave marker in a cemetery near Wetumpka, Alabama, captures this truth succinctly:

Here lies the body of Solomon Peas,
Under the grass and under the trees;
But Peas is not here, only the pod,
Peas shelled out and went to God.

For a believer, at death the real person, the soul/spirit of man, shells out of the pod and goes to be with the Lord. The body falls asleep and is placed in the ground. At the Rapture, the body will be raised incorruptible and immortal and joined to the perfected spirit (1 Thessalonians 4:14–16).

For the unbeliever, things could not be more different. When an unbeliever dies, his or her departed spirit goes immediately into hades to experience conscious, unrelenting torment. In Luke 16:19–31, when the unbelieving rich man died, his soul was transported instantly to hades: "The rich man also died and was buried. In Hades he lifted up his eyes, being in torment, and saw Abraham far away and Lazarus in his bosom" (vv. 22–23).

Make no mistake. Death is not the end. It's the beginning of an eternal existence in one of two places. Death is followed by a destination. But while death does not end our existence, it does end many things.

Dr. Walter C. Wilson was a Kansas City physician who taught the Bible and led evangelistic crusades. He once talked to an atheist who said, "Dr. Wilson, I don't believe what you're preaching." Wilson replied, "You have told me what you don't believe; perhaps you will tell me what you do believe."

"I do believe that death ends all," the man maintained.

"So do I," Wilson replied.

"What! You believe death ends all?"

"I certainly do," he answered. "Death ends all your chances of doing evil; death ends all your joy; death ends all of your projects, all your ambitions, all your friendships; death ends all the gospel you will ever hear; death ends it all for you, and you must go into outer darkness.

"As for myself, death ends all my wanderings, all my tears, all my perplexities, all my disappointments, all my aches and pains; death ends it all, and I will go to be with my Lord in glory."

"I never thought of it that way," the atheist said. Walter Wilson then led the man to faith in Jesus Christ, after agreeing with him that death ends it all.

Maybe you've never thought of it that way, either. It's something to consider.

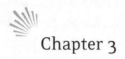

Chapter 3

IS THERE AN APPOINTED TIME TO DIE?

A visitor asked an old-timer, "What's the death rate around here?"

"Same as back east," the old-timer drawled, "one to a person."

The Bible clearly teaches that death is an appointment for every person. "And inasmuch as it is appointed for men to die once and after this comes judgment" (Hebrews 9:27). We are all painfully aware of our mortality.

But more specifically, people often want to know if there is an *exact* appointed time for each person to die. I believe the Bible teaches that God has indeed set that date for each of us, and it cannot be changed. The Creator has allotted us a fixed number of days and hours on this earth.

In Job, the oldest book in the Bible, we read these words: "Since his days are determined, the number of his months is with

You; and his limits You have set so that he cannot pass" (14:5). Ultimately, God declares Himself the One who gives life and takes life. "See now that I, I am He, and there is no god besides Me; it is I who put to death and give life. I have wounded, and it is I who heal; and there is no one who can deliver from My hand" (Deuteronomy 32:39).

Psalm 139:16 says, "All the days ordained for me were written in your book before one of them came to be" (NIV).

I don't believe this means that God is the direct cause of every death that occurs. People often die as a result of the sin of others. For instance, people are murdered, killed by terrorists, killed by drunk drivers, or die as a result of someone else's negligence. God is not the author or initiator of human sin. But what this does indicate is that ultimately everything is under God's control—which is just another way of saying that God is sovereign. He runs His universe.

In Revelation 11 we read about two men known as the "two witnesses" who will live during the coming Tribulation period of the end times. The Antichrist will hate these two men and try to kill them repeatedly, but God will supernaturally protect their lives. At some point, however, God will allow them to be slain. Verse 7 says, "When they have finished their testimony, the beast that comes up out of the abyss will make war with them, and overcome them and kill them."

Did you catch that? God will only allow them to be killed "when they have finished their testimony."

I believe it's the same for every believer. We are immortal until we have finished the work God has for us to accomplish. But when that work is done (and only God knows when that time comes for each person), God calls us home.

Another question you might be asking at this point is: "How does exercise and eating right fit in with this idea that everyone has an appointed time to die? Won't I live longer if I take care of myself?" I have to admit that I'm not really sure how all this fits together in the plan of God. But certainly the sovereign God who knows all things factors everything into our divine appointment with death.

What we *can* say from Scripture is that death is an appointment you and I must keep. No death is an "accident" from God's perspective. This should give us great comfort when a loved one or friend departs this life. It's a part of God's sovereign plan for that person. It may not have been the time we would have chosen, but it was God's time. And while we may not understand His timing, it's a comfort to know that a loving Creator is working out His perfect plan for our lives and this world.

In his short story "The Appointment in Samara," W. Somerset Maugham makes the point that our appointment with death will always be right on time. In his tale, he tells of a certain merchant in Baghdad who sent his servant to the market to buy some provisions. A little while later, the servant returned, looking white in the face. In a trembling voice he said, "Just now in the marketplace I was jostled by a man in the crowd, and when I turned I saw it was Mr. Death. He looked at me and made a threatening gesture. Please lend me your horse, because I want to go to Samara where Mr. Death will not be able to find me."

The merchant agreed and lent the terrified man his horse. The servant mounted the horse and rode away as fast as the animal could gallop. Later that day, the merchant went down to the marketplace and saw Mr. Death standing in the crowd. He approached him and said, "Why did you make a threatening gesture to my servant when you saw him this morning?"

"That was not a threatening gesture," said Mr. Death. "It was only a start of surprise. I was astonished to see him in Baghdad because I have an appointment with him tonight in Samara."

Poet Alan Seeger expressed this truth poignantly in his famous work "I Have a Rendezvous with Death":

> I have a rendezvous with Death
> At some disputed barricade,
> When Spring comes back with rustling shade
> And apple-blossoms fill the air—
> I have a rendezvous with Death
> When Spring brings back blue days and fair.
>
> It may be he shall take my hand
> And lead me into his dark land
> And close my eyes and quench my breath—
> It may be I shall pass him still.
> I have a rendezvous with Death
> On some scarred slope of battered hill,
> When Spring comes round again this year
> And the first meadow-flowers appear.
>
> God knows 'twere better to be deep
> Pillowed in silk and scented down,
> Where love throbs out in blissful sleep,
> Pulse nigh to pulse, and breath to breath,
> Where hushed awakenings are dear…
> But I've a rendezvous with Death
> At midnight in some flaming town,
> When Spring trips north again this year,
> And I to my pledged word am true,
> I shall not fail that rendezvous.

Our God, who loves us more than we can begin to imagine, remains in charge of the timing of our rendezvous with death. With the psalmist we can restfully say, "My times are in Your hand" (Psalm 31:15).

Chapter 4

WILL EVERYBODY DIE?

George Bernard Shaw once observed, "One out of one people die."

Of course, Shaw's wry observation was nothing new. The Bible, in Hebrews 9:27, says, "And inasmuch as it is appointed for men to die once and after this comes judgment."

This verse establishes the general truth that all must die. And everyone has...with two notable exceptions. Both Enoch (Genesis 5:24) and Elijah (2 Kings 2:11) were caught up to heaven without tasting physical death.

Will they be the only exceptions? Far from it! There will be millions of exceptions to this general rule at a great event called the Rapture, when all believers in Jesus Christ who are alive at that time will be immediately translated to heaven without tasting physical death.

The Rapture: A Biblical Teaching

A few years ago I was in a restaurant having lunch with a man who had just started attending our church. He had asked me some questions about the end times, and I began describing to him the coming Rapture of the church. In the middle of our conversation a man at the table next to us—who had obviously been eavesdropping—spoke out sharply. He told me in no uncertain terms that the Rapture was an unbiblical doctrine because the word *rapture* wasn't even in the Bible.

The man was right. And he was also dead wrong.

While he was wrong in denying the doctrine of the Rapture, he was absolutely correct in stating that the word *rapture* is not in the English translations of the Bible.

If you were to read all of the 774,747 words (plus or minus) in the King James Version of the Bible or in any other well-known translation, you would not find the word *rapture*. At the same time, you would also look in vain for the words *Trinity, Bible,* or *grandfather*. And yet we know that all of these things are very real and true.

In 1 Thessalonians 4:17, the words "caught up" are a translation of the Greek word *harpazo,* which means to snatch, to seize, or to take away. This same word is used in several other New Testament passages that convey the idea of being "caught up" or "snatched away." In each of these verses I have italicized the word that translates *harpazo* so you can see how it's used.

> "My Father, who has given them to Me, is greater than all; and no one is able to *snatch* them out of the Father's hand." (John 10:29)

When they came up out of the water, the Spirit of the Lord *snatched* Philip away; and the eunuch no longer saw him, but went on his way rejoicing. (Acts 8:39)

I know a man in Christ who fourteen years ago—whether in the body I do not know, or out of the body I do not know, God knows—such a man was *caught up* to the third heaven. And I know how such a man—whether in the body or apart from the body I do not know, God knows—was *caught up* into Paradise and heard inexpressible words, which a man is not permitted to speak. (2 Corinthians 12:2–4)

While you won't find the word *rapture* in any English translations of 1 Thessalonians 4:17, you will find it in the Latin translation of the Bible produced by Jerome in the early A.D. 400s. This translation, known as the Vulgate, served as the main Bible of the western medieval church until the Reformation. In the Vulgate, Jerome translated the Greek word *harpazo* in 1 Thessalonians 4:17 with the word *raeptius,* which was brought over to English as *rapture.*

So although the word *rapture* does not occur in most English translations, the concept or doctrine of a catching away of living believers to meet the Lord is clearly stated in 1 Corinthians 15:51–55 and 1 Thessalonians 4:17. This doctrine could just as well be called the "catching away of the church," "the snatching away of the church," the "translation of the church," or the "*harpazo* of the church." But since the phrase "Rapture of the church" is an excellent description of this event and has become the most common title, there is no reason to change the terminology.

THE KEY RAPTURE PASSAGES

While the New Testament refers to the Rapture many times, three main passages actually describe that event. Reading each of these passages will give you a basic overview of the Rapture, directly from Scripture.

"Do not let your heart be troubled; believe in God, believe also in Me. In My Father's house are many dwelling places; if it were not so, I would have told you; for I go to prepare a place for you. If I go and prepare place for you, I will come again and receive you to Myself, that where I am, there you may be also." (John 14:1–3)

Now I say this, brethren, that flesh and blood cannot inherit the kingdom of God; nor does the perishable inherit the imperishable. Behold, I tell you a mystery; we will not all sleep, but we will all be changed, in a moment, in the twinkling of an eye, at the last trumpet; for the trumpet will sound, and the dead will be raised imperishable, and we will be changed. For this perishable must put on the imperishable, and this mortal must put on immortality. But when this perishable will have put on the imperishable, and this mortal will have put on immortality, then will come about the saying that is written, "Death is swallowed up in victory. O death, where is your victory? O death, where is your sting?" The sting of death is sin, and the power of sin is the law; but thanks be to God, who gives us the victory through our Lord Jesus Christ. (1 Corinthians 15:50–57)

But we do not want you to be uninformed, brethren, about those who are asleep, so that you will not grieve as do the rest who have no hope. For if we believe that Jesus died and rose again, even so God will bring with Him those who have fallen asleep in Jesus. For this we say to you by the word of the Lord, that we who are alive and remain until the coming of the Lord, will not precede those who have fallen asleep. For the Lord Himself will descend from heaven with a shout, with the voice of the archangel and with the trumpet of God, and the dead in Christ will rise first. Then we who are alive and remain will be caught up together with them in the clouds to meet the Lord in the air, and so we shall always be with the Lord. Therefore comfort one another with these words. (1 Thessalonians 4:13–18)

DEFINING THE RAPTURE

The Rapture is that future event when in a moment of time, in the blink of an eye, every true believer in Jesus Christ as their personal Savior will be physically transported up into the clouds to meet Jesus, then from there return with Him to His Father's house in heaven.

All this will happen within a split second of time and will occur before the onset of the horrifying seven-year Tribulation. At the same instant, the raptured believer will undergo the transformation of his or her current physical body into a new physical body, equipped to live forever with God in heaven. In conjunction with this astounding event will be the resurrection of all believers who have lived and died on earth within the two thousand years of the church age. They too will be given new bodies fit for heaven.

Both groups will meet Christ in the air and go to the Father's house in their new resurrection bodies to be with Jesus forever. The Rapture is the blessed hope of the church.

There are seven key points in 1 Thessalonians 4:13–18 that summarize the precious truth of the Rapture.

1. The Realization (vv. 13–14)

> But we do not want you to be uninformed, brethren, about those who are asleep, so that you will not grieve as do the rest who have no hope. For if we believe that Jesus died and rose again, even so God will bring with Him those who have fallen asleep in Jesus.

At the outset, Paul makes it clear that he wants us to understand the Rapture. Notice these important words: "But we do not want you to be uninformed, brethren." The Lord wants every believer to know the truth of the Rapture. In the King James Version of the Bible, verse 13 begins, "But I would not have you to be ignorant, brethren...." Someone once said that the fastest-growing denomination in America is the "church of the ignorant brethren." But the Lord doesn't want us to be ignorant about the truth of the Rapture.

The first thing the Lord wants us to realize about the Rapture is that our believing loved ones who have passed away will not miss out on that great event. When Jesus returns, He will bring the perfected spirits of departed believers with Him. Knowing this truth brings comfort and hope to our hearts and softens our grieving when loved ones pass away. When believers pass away, it is not good-bye, but only good night. We will see them again at the Rapture.

2. The Revelation (v. 15a)

Paul also wants us to know without any doubt that what he is saying is directly from the Lord: "For this we say to you by the word of the Lord." What Paul is recording is divinely revealed. It's not something he made up on his own.

3. The Return (15b–16)

> ...that we who are alive and remain until the coming of the Lord, will not precede those who have fallen asleep. For the Lord Himself will descend from heaven with a shout, with the voice of the archangel and with the trumpet of God, and the dead in Christ will rise first.

At the Rapture, the Lord Himself will come again in the clouds. He will return accompanied by three things: a commanding shout, the call of the archangel, and the trumpet call of God.

This commanding shout is the last of three great cries or commands of the Savior: (1) the cry from the cemetery when Lazarus was raised (John 11:43–44); (2) the cry from the cross when the dead came to life (Matthew 27:50–53); (3) the cry from the clouds when the dead are raised at His coming (1 Thessalonians 4:16). Notice that at each of these cries the dead are resurrected.

4. The Resurrection (16b)

> ...and the dead in Christ will rise first.

When Christ comes down from heaven, the first thing that will happen is that the bodies of deceased believers will be raised, or resurrected, and reunited to their perfected spirits that have returned with the Lord. These resurrected bodies will be glorified, incorruptible bodies fit for the heavenly realm (1 Corinthians 15:35–56; 2 Corinthians 5:1–5; Philippians 3:20–21).

Someone has said that the reason the dead will be raised first is because they have six feet farther to go.

5. The Removal (17a)

> Then we who are alive and remain will be caught up together with them in the clouds.

When the dead have been raised, living believers will immediately be transformed and translated into the presence of the Christ without ever tasting physical death. As 1 Corinthians 15:51 says, "Not all of us will die, but we will all be transformed" (NLT). The King James Version states: "We shall not all sleep, but we shall all be changed." This verse is often mounted on the door of church nurseries. It's certainly true of many children in a church nursery, but thanks be to God, it will be true of millions of His children when the Savior descends from heaven. Millions of believers will never face the sting of death, but will be removed or raptured directly into the presence of the Lord in the clouds. This translation will take place in the amount of time it takes to blink one's eye (v. 52).

In 1 Corinthians 15:51, the apostle Paul refers to the Rapture as a "mystery." When we think of a mystery we most often think of a story or event that is difficult to understand or solve. But in the New Testament a mystery is a truth that God reveals for the first time.

Paul was God's chosen vessel to reveal the mystery of the Rapture. "Behold, I shew you a mystery; we shall not all sleep, but we shall all be changed" (v. 51, KJV). The mystery of the

Rapture is that some people will go to heaven and receive new, glorified bodies without ever dying. They will do an end run on the grave.

This was a totally new truth that had never been disclosed by God until 1 Corinthians 15. If you read in your Bible from Genesis 1 to all the way through to 1 Corinthians 14, you would correctly conclude that the only way to get to heaven would be to die.

But in 1 Corinthians 15 that all changes.

Through the pen of His apostle, the Lord unveils this glorious mystery that a whole generation of believers will be transformed without tasting the sting of physical death. In a fraction of a millisecond, millions of believers will find themselves in brand-new, perfect, live-forever bodies. This is the glorious mystery of the Rapture. May we be the generation to experience this breath-taking event!

6. The Reunion (17)

The dead in Christ and the living saints will all be raptured together and will meet the Lord in the air. What a glorious reunion as all the saints of this age meet the dear Savior and see Him face-to-face.

7. The Reassurance (18)

Therefore comfort one another with these words.

One very practical application of the Rapture is that it brings comfort and hope to God's people when a believing loved one or friend goes home to be with the Lord. Those who have died in Christ will be raised. And we will be reunited with them in heaven. These words have certainly been read at thousands of funerals throughout the centuries and have brought the comfort, hope, and encouragement of the Lord to broken, bereaved hearts.

CONCLUSION

When will this event called the Rapture occur? No man knows the day or the hour. It's an event that from the human perspective could occur at any moment. It could happen today. Make sure you are ready when the Savior comes.

Make sure you are Rapture-ready!

You don't want to be left behind to face the Great Tribulation.

Chapter 5

IS PURGATORY REAL?

The Roman Catholic Church and the Greek Orthodox Church teach that the vast majority of believers do not go immediately to heaven when they die. They believe that they go to a place called purgatory. It's believed that most Christians are not bad enough to go to hell, but neither are they good enough to be candidates for heaven.

Therefore, something has to happen in between.

That something is a place called purgatory, where deceased believers suffer anguish and are thereby gradually purged or purified.[5]

In order to understand the notion of purgatory, let's consider three main points:

1. The definition of purgatory—*what* is it?
2. The defense of purgatory—*how* do people support it?
3. The difficulties of purgatory—*why* should we reject it?

The Definition: *What* Is It?

The word purgatory comes from a Latin word that means "to purge." Zachary J. Hayes, a Catholic scholar, defines purgatory as follows:

> The word is commonly understood to refer to the state, place, or condition in the next world between heaven and hell, a state of purifying suffering for those who have died and are still in need of such purification.... Purgatory, as Roman Catholic theology envisions it, involves the process of purification after death for those who need it. It is a process in which the concern of the living for the dead, expressed through prayers and charitable works, may have a beneficial effect on the healing of the dead.... Some sort of a cleansing process is postulated between death and the entrance into heaven.[6]

Cardinal Ratzinger describes purgatory like this:

> Purgatory means that there is some unresolved guilt in the person who has died. Hence there is a suffering which continues to radiate because of the guilt. In this sense, purgatory means suffering to the end what one has left behind on earth—in the certainty of being accepted, yet having to bear the burden of the withdrawn presence of the Beloved.[7]

Lorraine Boettner, a Protestant scholar, gives this excellent description of purgatory in the *Evangelical Dictionary of Theology*:

The teachings of the Roman Catholic and Greek Orthodox churches set forth a place of temporal punishment in the intermediate realm known as purgatory, in which it is held that all those who die at peace with the church but who are not perfect must undergo penal and purifying suffering. Only those believers who have attained a state of Christian perfection are said to go immediately to heaven. All unbaptized adults and those who after baptism have committed mortal sin go immediately to hell. The great mass of partially sanctified Christians dying in fellowship with the church but nevertheless encumbered with some degree of sin go to purgatory where, for a longer or shorter time, they suffer until all sin is purged away, after which they are translated to heaven.

The sufferings vary greatly in intensity and duration, being proportioned in general to the guilt and impurity or impenitence of the sufferer. They are described as being in some cases comparatively mild, lasting perhaps only a few hours, while in other cases little if anything short of the torments of hell and lasting for thousands of years. But in any event they are to terminate with the last judgment. Gifts or services rendered to the church, prayers by the priests, and Masses provided by relatives or friends in behalf of the deceased can shorten, alleviate, or eliminate the sojourn of the soul in purgatory.[8]

The gist of this teaching is that there are two kinds of sin: mortal and venial. Mortal sins are really bad sins that are called mortal because they have the power to kill grace in a person's life. Grace can die. If a person commits a mortal sin they must be restored through the sacrament of Penance or else perish forever. All other regular sins are venial (forgivable) sins.

Purgatory, then, is a kind of halfway house or state of limbo between heaven and hell where believers must finish paying for their venial sins. Part of the belief in purgatory is that the person who ends up there is unable to do anything on his own to shorten his time. Time in purgatory depends on two things: the kind of life the person lived on earth and what his friends on earth are doing for him. It's believed that those who are alive on earth can help out their friends and relatives who are in purgatory by praying for them, having Masses done on their behalf, and even by obtaining or purchasing indulgences. An indulgence is a remission of either all or part of the temporal punishment due for sin. It's believed that the pope exercises some kind of jurisdiction over purgatory. It is his prerogative, by granting indulgences, to lighten the anguish of the soul in purgatory or even terminate it altogether.

In fairness, it should be recognized that since the Second Vatican Council, indulgences have played a less significant role in the spiritual life of the Roman Catholic Church. Nevertheless, it was greatly abused in the past and remains part of Roman Catholic dogma to this day.

Indulgences were one of the main ways the church raised revenue. They were "certificates" produced in bulk that had been pre-signed by the pope and pardoned a person's sins and granted access to heaven. So, if you knew you had sinned, you would wait until a pardoner was in your region selling an indulgence and purchase one. You would do this believing that the pope, as God's representative on earth, would forgive your sins and you would be pardoned. This industry was later extended to allow people to purchase an indulgence for a dead relative who might be in purgatory, to relieve that relative of the temporal punishment for his sins. In doing this you would be viewed by the Catholic Church as committing a Christian act, thereby elevating your status in the eyes of God.

The granting of indulgences for money to release people from purgatory was one of Martin Luther's main problems with the Roman Catholic Church, prompting his Ninety-Five Theses and the birth of the Protestant Reformation. It was taught in that day that for one-fourth of a florin, buyers were assured that "as soon as the coin the coffer rings, the soul from purgatory springs."

THE DEFENSE: *HOW* DO PEOPLE SUPPORT IT?

Catholic scholars honestly admit that the real support for purgatory comes from church tradition, not the Bible. However, they do point to several passages to bolster their view.

The primary support for the doctrine of purgatory comes from the apocryphal book of 2 Maccabees, chapter 12, verses 39–45. The Apocrypha is a collection of fifteen books written during the intertestamental period (the time between the Old and New Testaments) that is included in the Roman Catholic and Greek Orthodox Bibles, but is excluded from Protestant Bibles.

In context, the 2 Maccabees passage refers to the actions of a Jewish hero named Judas Maccabeus, and some of his soldiers after a battle. The text says:

> On the next day, as by that time it had become necessary, Judas and his men went to take up the bodies of the fallen and to bring them back to lie with their kinsman in the sepulchers of their fathers. Then under the tunic of every one of the dead they found sacred tokens of the idols of Jamnia, which the law forbids the Jews to wear. And it became clear to all that this was why these men had fallen. So they all blessed the ways of the Lord, the Righteous Judge, who reveals the things that are hidden;

and they turned to prayer, beseeching that the sin which had been committed might be wholly blotted out. And the noble Judas exhorted the people to keep themselves free from sin, for they had seen with their own eyes what had happened because of the sin of those who had fallen. He also took up a collection, man by man, to the amount of two thousand drachmas of silver, and sent it to Jerusalem to provide for a sin offering. In doing this he acted very well and honorably, taking into account the resurrection. For if he were not expecting that those who had fallen would rise again, it would have been superfluous and foolish to pray for the dead. But if he was looking to the splendid reward that is laid up for those who fall asleep in godliness, it was a holy and pious thought. Therefore, he made atonement for the dead that they might be delivered from their sin.

There are three main problems with using this passage to support purgatory. First, 2 Maccabees is an apocryphal book that is not part of the Old Testament canon of Scripture recognized by Jesus and the apostles. The books of the Apocrypha were not accepted as Scripture in any of the early church councils, nor were they quoted as Scripture by the early church fathers. Therefore, the books in the Apocrypha are neither divinely inspired nor authoritative.

Second, the passage never mentions a place called purgatory. In this passage Judas and his soldiers pray and offer sacrifices on behalf of their fallen comrades for the sin of idolatry, but there is no clear development of any teaching of a specific place called purgatory. To build an extensive doctrine of purgatory based primarily on this one passage (which doesn't even teach it) is tenuous and irresponsible at best...and heretical at worst.

Third, in the 2 Maccabees account, the soldiers who died committed the sin of idolatry. Judas found an idol of Jamnia in the tunic of every dead soldier. He believed this rebellion against God was the cause of their death. It's interesting, however, that Roman Catholics use this passage to support the doctrine of purgatory since idolatry is a mortal sin that makes one ineligible for purgatory! According to Catholic teaching, anyone who commits a mortal sin is sent straight to hell unless he is restored by the sacrament of Penance. So even if this text taught of a place called purgatory (which I don't believe it does), it would negate the application of it to these dead soldiers because of the nature of the sin involved and their lack of Penance.

Those who believe in purgatory also point to four New Testament passages to support their teaching. Here are the four texts and a brief comment on each one.

(1) "Truly I say to you, you will not come out of there until you have paid up the last cent." (Matthew 5:26)

The context for this verse in Matthew's Gospel makes it clear that this is talking about a man being thrown into prison on earth and paying his financial debt, not paying his spiritual debt in purgatory.

(2) "Whoever speaks a word against the Son of Man, it shall be forgiven him; but whoever speaks against the Holy Spirit, it shall not be forgiven him, either in this age or in the age to come." (Matthew 12:32)

This text, describing what is commonly called the "unpardonable sin," discusses the particular unique sin of the leaders in that first-century generation in Israel who visibly saw the person and works of Jesus Christ and assigned His works to Satan. Jesus said that the sin of that generation would not be forgiven. This clearly has nothing to do with purgatory since allegedly in purgatory sin can ultimately be forgiven.

> (3) "And his lord, moved with anger, handed him over to the torturers until he should repay all that was owed him." (Matthew 18:34)

In the context of this parable about forgiving others, the torture is in *this* life, not the life to come. The one who fails to forgive others is turned over to the emotional and mental anguish and torture of his own unforgiving heart.

> (4) Each man's work will become evident; for the day will show it because it is to be revealed with fire, and the fire itself will test the quality of each man's work. If any man's work which he has built on it remains, he will receive a reward. If any man's work is burned up, he will suffer loss; but he himself will be saved, yet so as through fire. (1 Corinthians 3:13–15)

The context of this passage is the local church at Corinth. Paul and others had laid the spiritual foundation of the church, which was Jesus Christ (1 Corinthians 3:9–11).

Now others at Corinth were building the superstructure on the foundation. If they used gold, silver, and precious stones (things of value that will last), they would receive a reward from God. But if they built with wood, hay, and straw (worthless things that won't last), their works would be burned up when they stood before the Lord someday.

Paul mentions this event, known as the judgment seat of

Christ, three other times in his Corinthian correspondence (1 Corinthians 4:5; 9:24–27; 2 Corinthians 5:10). It's a time of accounting and evaluation that each believer will face for a divine appraisal of how we lived our life after we trusted Jesus Christ as our Savior from sin. It has nothing to do with purgatory. Worthless works will be burned up, not the person.

THE DIFFICULTIES—*WHY* SHOULD WE REJECT IT?

The doctrine of purgatory has several serious problems, as we have already noted, but two main difficulties stand out.

First, belief in purgatory reveals a serious misunderstanding of the biblical doctrine of salvation. Clearly, man desperately needs purging from his sins. But the Bible says that this cleansing comes through the blood of Jesus Christ, not the purgatorial fires. "The blood of Jesus His Son cleanses us from all sin" (1 John 1:7b). According to God's Word, we are justified or declared righteous before God by Christ's merit alone, through faith alone, and not in any way by our own works (Romans 4:5; 5:1; Ephesians 2:8–9; Titus 3:5).

In the bookkeeping of heaven, when Christ died on the cross all our sin was imputed to Him, or credited to His account. God is the Master Certified Accountant. When we trust Christ as our Savior, God transfers our sin from our debt column and places it in Christ's debt column. And then Christ's righteousness is placed in our credit column in the books of heaven. Second Corinthians 5:21 says it best: "He made Him who knew no sin to be sin on our behalf, so that we might become the righteousness of God in Him." What a transaction! He took my sin, and I get His righteousness.

For this reason, there is absolutely no reason for any true Christian to ever spend one second in a place called purgatory. All our sins have been washed away, and we have a perfect standing before God in Jesus Christ. There is absolutely "no condemnation for those who are in Christ Jesus" (Romans 8:1). We are totally prepared for heaven from the very moment we trust in Christ. We are never prepared in ourselves. Our perfect standing before God is in Jesus Christ.

As Hebrew 10:14 says, "For by one offering He has perfected for all time those who are sanctified."

The doctrine of purgatory exposes the false belief that salvation is really by faith *plus* works. In purgatory, man pays his own bill. He endures punishment for his own sin. Proponents of purgatory believe the formula for salvation looks like this:

Faith + Works = Salvation

In contrast, the biblical teaching concerning salvation is:

Faith = Salvation + Works

Ephesians 2:8–10 says, "For by grace you have been saved through faith; and that not of yourselves, it is the gift of God; not as a result of works, that no one may boast. For we are His workmanship, created in Christ Jesus for good works, which God prepared beforehand so that we would walk in them."

In other words, we do good works because we *are* saved from our sins, not to *get* saved. Good works are the fruit, product, or evidence of salvation, not the cause of it.

Salvation is *by* grace,

through faith,

unto or *for* good works.

The doctrine of purgatory contradicts the Bible teaching of the finished work of Jesus on the cross for human sin and the biblical teaching of salvation.

Here's a second fatal flaw in the doctrine of purgatory: The clear teaching of Scripture makes it plain that when a true believer in Jesus Christ dies, he or she enjoys immediate, conscious, personal fellowship with Him—with no mention of a stopping-off place in between. Consider these two verses.

> We are of good courage, I say, and prefer rather to be absent from the body and to be at home with the Lord. (2 Corinthians 5:8)

> But I am hard-pressed from both directions, having the desire to depart and be with Christ, for that is very much better. (Philippians 1:23)

Think about it. If Paul expected to go to purgatory when he died to face the purgatorial fires, that would hardly have been preferable to continuing to live this life.

For that matter, according to Philippians 3:20, every believer is already a citizen of heaven—right now! "For our citizenship is in heaven, from which also we eagerly wait for a Savior, the Lord Jesus Christ."

For all who have come to Jesus in simple faith, trusting Him alone for salvation, death will usher us immediately into the presence of the Lord. We will see Him face-to-face.

What a comforting promise!

Chapter 6

SHOULD WE PRAY FOR THOSE WHO HAVE DIED?

Many Christians have been taught that it is their responsibility to pray either *for* or *to* those who have already died. Millions around the world offer prayers for the departed, hoping to somehow shorten their stay in purgatory, or help them on their way in the afterlife. At the same time, prayers are directed to departed believers, often called saints, in hope that these men and women on the other side will help those who pray on their journey through life on earth.

Both of these practices are completely unbiblical. The Bible never once calls on believers to pray either *for* the dead or *to* the dead.

Yes, Scripture calls on believers to prayer for the "saints" (Ephesians 6:18). But *every* true believer in Jesus Christ is a saint ("set-apart one") in Jesus Christ. Praying for the saints in the

New Testament refers to praying for believers who are still alive.

Those who have died and gone to heaven don't need our prayers. They are with Jesus Christ in glory. Why would they need our prayers? And those who have died and gone to hades are there forever. There is no way of escape for them or lessening of their suffering. So there is no reason to pray for them either.

Rather than spending time in prayer for those who have departed this life, use your time in prayer wisely to pray for temporal and spiritual needs for yourself, your family, your friends, your church, and your government leaders. These are prayers that will really make a difference.

Chapter 7

WHAT ABOUT SOUL SLEEP?

Several groups today, including Seventh Day Adventists and Jehovah's Witnesses, adhere to a teaching called "soul sleep." In earlier times, some Anabaptists also endorsed this teaching. The technical term for this doctrine is *psychopannychy*. The doctrine of soul sleep maintains that when a person dies, the soul, as well as the body, sleeps in the grave unconscious until the resurrection. In other words, the body returns to dust while the soul becomes unconscious.

Soul sleep deals with the time commonly known as the intermediate state—the time between physical death and the resurrection of the body at the Rapture.

Soul sleep is based on two key thoughts. First, human existence demands unity of body and soul. And second, the idea of sleep, which is used of the dead in the Bible, indicates loss of consciousness.

The main biblical support for the doctrine of soul sleep is

found in several Old Testament verses. In Ecclesiastes 3:20 we read, "All go to the same place. All came from the dust and all return to the dust." This verse is talking about man's body that returns to dust, not his soul. The next verse makes this clear and states that at death the soul leaves the body. "Who knows that the breath of man ascends upward and the breath of the beast descends downward to the earth?"

The main verse used by advocates of soul sleep is Ecclesiastes 9:5: "For the living know they will die; but the dead do not know anything, nor have they any longer a reward, for their memory is forgotten."

Two major problems arise when you try to use this verse to prove soul sleep. First, the book of Ecclesiastes frequently states things that only *appear* to be true from the human perspective—from the limited vantage point of "life under the sun."

Second, interpreting Ecclesiastes 9:5 in this way can't be harmonized with other statements made in the same book. Solomon clearly believed that the soul continues on in conscious existence after death. He writes, for instance, "Then the dust will return to the earth as it was, and the spirit will return to God who gave it" (Ecclesiastes 12:7).

Another key verse for soul sleep advocates is Daniel 12:2: "Many of those who sleep in the dust of the ground will awake, these to everlasting life, but the others to disgrace and everlasting contempt." Again, the sleep spoken of in this passage refers not to the soul but to the body. It is true that the body falls asleep at the moment of physical death. It's the body that will be resurrected or "awakened" in the end times.

Eleven explicit passages in Scripture refute the false teaching of soul sleep.

1. Genesis 35:18: "It came about as her soul was departing (for she died), that she named him Ben-oni; but his father called him Benjamin." Notice, Rachel's soul didn't sink into unconsciousness; it departed. It went somewhere.

2. First Samuel 28:13–15a:

> The king said to her, "'Do not be afraid; but what do you see?" And the woman said to Saul, "I see a divine being coming up out of the earth." He said to her, "What is his form?" And she said, "An old man is coming up, and he is wrapped with a robe." And Saul knew that it was Samuel, and he bowed with his face to the ground and did homage. Then Samuel said to Saul, "Why have you disturbed me by bringing me up?"

Samuel the prophet, who had already died, was conscious and aware of what was transpiring.

3. Matthew 17:1–3:

> "Six days later Jesus took with Him Peter and James and John his brother, and led them up on a high mountain by themselves. And He was transfigured before them; and His face shone like the sun, and His garments became as white as light. And behold, Moses and Elijah appeared to them, talking with Him."

Moses had been dead for about fourteen hundred years, and Elijah had been raptured to heaven about eight hundred years before. During Jesus' earthly ministry they appear with Him on the Mount of Transfiguration. Their souls were far from unconscious!

4. Matthew 27:52: "The tombs were opened, and many bodies of the saints who had fallen asleep were raised." It was the bodies that were asleep, and then raised.

5. Luke 16:19-31:

"There was a rich man who was dressed in purple and fine linen and lived in luxury every day. At his gate was laid a beggar named Lazarus, covered with sores and longing to eat what fell from the rich man's table. Even the dogs came and licked his sores.

"The time came when the beggar died and the angels carried him to Abraham's side. The rich man also died and was buried. In hell [hades], where he was in torment, he looked up and saw Abraham far away, with Lazarus by his side. So he called to him, 'Father Abraham, have pity on me and send Lazarus to dip the tip of his finger in water and cool my tongue, because I am in agony in this fire.'

"But Abraham replied, 'Son, remember that in your lifetime you received your good things, while Lazarus received bad things, but now he is comforted here and you are in agony. And besides all this, between us and you a great chasm has been fixed, so that those who want to go from here to you cannot, nor can anyone cross over from there to us.'

"He answered, 'Then I beg you, father, send Lazarus to my father's house, for I have five brothers. Let him warn them, so that they will not also come to this place of torment.'

"Abraham replied, 'They have Moses and the Prophets; let them listen to them.'

"'No, father Abraham,' he said, 'but if someone from the dead goes to them, they will repent.'

"He said to him, 'If they do not listen to Moses and the Prophets, they will not be convinced even if someone rises from the dead" (NIV).

When they died, the souls of both the rich man and Lazarus continued in conscious existence. The rich man in hades could see, hear, speak, and feel.

6. *Luke 23:39–43:*

One of the criminals who were hanged there was hurling abuse at Him, saying, "Are You not the Christ? Save Yourself and us!" But the other answered, and rebuking him said, "Do you not even fear God, since you are under the same sentence of condemnation? And we indeed are suffering justly, for we are receiving what we deserve for our deeds; but this man has done nothing wrong." And he was saying, "Jesus, remember me when You come in Your kingdom!" And He said to him, "Truly I say to you, today you shall be with Me in Paradise."

Jesus promised the repentant thief that when he died he would be with Him in Paradise that very day.

7. *Acts 7:56, 59–60:*

And he said, "Behold, I see the heavens opened up and the Son of Man standing at the right hand of God." They went on stoning Stephen as he called on the Lord and said, "Lord Jesus, receive my spirit!" Then falling on his knees, he cried out with a loud voice, "Lord, do not hold this sin against them!" Having said this, he fell asleep.

This is the only time the Bible refers to Jesus "standing at the right hand of God." Every other time Jesus is sitting at God's right hand. Jesus stood up to welcome His faithful servant Stephen to heaven. Stephen's body fell asleep, but he asked the Lord to receive his spirit at the moment of death.

8. *Second Corinthians 5:8:* "We are of good courage, I say, and prefer rather to be absent from the body and to be at home with the Lord."

Absence from the body is immediate presence with the Lord.

9. *Philippians 1:23:* "But I am hard-pressed from both directions, having the desire to depart and be with Christ, for that is very much better."

Death for the believer is departing to be with Christ.

10. *Second Peter 2:9:* "Then the Lord knows how to rescue the godly from temptation, and to keep the unrighteous under punishment for the day of judgment."

This verse says that the lost are undergoing punishment presently as they await the day of judgment. Even the souls of departed unbelievers aren't asleep.

11. *Revelation 6:9–10:*

When the Lamb broke the fifth seal, I saw underneath the altar the souls of those who had been slain because of the word of God, and because of the testimony which they had maintained; and they cried out with a loud voice, saying, "How long, O Lord, holy and true, will You refrain from judging and avenging our blood on those who dwell on the earth?"

The souls of these Tribulation believers who have died are in heaven, crying out to the Lord for vindication.

In addition to these verses, in all three accounts when Jesus raised the dead He spoke to the person as if he or she was still conscious and aware (Luke 7:14; 8:54; John 11:43).

In summary, Scripture teaches that when a person dies, the body does fall asleep, but the "real person" is immediately transported either to heaven or hades. The souls of believers will rejoin their bodies at the Rapture (1 Thessalonians 4:13–18) to live with Christ forever in heaven, while the souls of unbelievers will be reunited with their bodies at the Great White Throne Judgment to suffer eternal torment (Revelation 20:11–15).

Chapter 8

WHAT ABOUT NEAR-DEATH EXPERIENCES?

Some of the bestselling books in the last decade are about near-death experiences, or NDEs. Books like *Embraced by the Light* and *Saved by the Light* have captured the attention of millions who want to peer behind the veil of death to get a sneak preview of the afterlife. The Internet contains a flood of books, articles, and opinion about NDEs. People everywhere seem to be fascinated by this phenomenon, which has only been systematically studied for about the last thirty years.

In a poll a few years ago, a consensus of near-death researchers and the Gallup poll discovered that about 13 million adults in the United States claim to have had an NDE with at least some of the typical features.[9] That's about 5 percent of the total population.

But are these NDEs real? Can people who claim to have them give us helpful information about life on the other side? About what heaven is really like?

While there are many opinions and much that could be said about NDEs (whole books have been devoted to the topic), two foundational points are indispensable to any consideration of this subject.

First, it is critical to note that they are called *near-death* experiences, not *death* or *afterlife* experiences. The fact that people came back from whatever state they were in is proof that they didn't really die. Why, then, should we put any stock in what they purport to tell us about the afterlife? After all, they were only near death, not dead. It's as ridiculous as a woman telling another woman about her "near-pregnancy experience." The idea is laughable. Everyone knows that you either are or you aren't! Likewise, you're either dead or you're not.

Experts make a clear distinction between clinical death, which is reversible, and biological death, which without divine intervention is irreversible. By their very nature, NDEs are experienced by people who are clinically, but not biologically, dead. At best, what people in this condition experience is the transition between life and death, not the final destination. I don't know about you, but I'm much more interested in what I will experience *after* death than what I will experience when I'm *near* death.

The only people who ever really came back from a state of biological death are the very few individuals in Scripture that the Lord or one of His prophets or disciples raised from the dead. And none of them wrote a book about their experience or hit the talk show circuit. As far as we know they never said anything about their experience. Even the apostle Paul, who was caught up to heaven on one occasion, did not reveal the things he saw there (2 Corinthians 12:1–5). Of all the people in the Bible, only the apostle John was given a vision of heaven and then permitted by God to tell us some of the details (Revelation 4–5; 21–22). But his revelation was in the form of a vision, not a near-death experience.

Second, if you are determined to put stock in what people experience in near-death situations, you must also keep in mind that they aren't all positive. Numerous accounts have been given by people who experienced sheer terror during their NDE. But these reports don't get nearly as much press as the positive ones.

Third, much of the idle speculation that is related from NDEs sounds more occultic and New Age than truly biblical. The most common description of NDEs is seeing a beautiful, bright light. Some experts attribute this phenomenon to chemicals that are released in the brain. While this medical explanation is possible, a more sinister explanation may also lie behind some of these experiences. The Bible says that since God is light, Satan disguises himself as an angel of light to deceive the unsuspecting (2 Corinthians 11:14). Wouldn't it be expected that the great deceiver would try to lead people who don't know Christ to believe that when they die everything will be great? Doesn't it make sense that Satan would seek to convince men and women that one's relationship to Christ has no bearing on seeing the great light and entering heaven? This is Satan's greatest lie. We shouldn't be surprised that he would use it in an experience like an NDE to give some people false security about their eternal destiny.

Fourth, the only reliable source of information about the afterlife is the Bible. Any experience people claim to have must ultimately be evaluated by the highest authority—the Word of God. And the Bible contains no record of NDEs, nor does it instruct us to seek information concerning the afterlife from them.

Let me make it clear. I'm not saying that every NDE is demonic. I believe many are due to chemicals released in the brain. I'm also not saying that having one makes you an evil person. And I'm also not saying that everyone who claims to have had one has a bad motive. I'm sure many people who have had them are true believers in Christ.

What I'm saying is that we should turn to God's Word as our sole authoritative source to discover what we want to know about the afterlife and be satisfied with what God has chosen to reveal to us about heaven and hell. Here's the real bottom line: NDEs really don't tell us anything about life after death.

Think about it like this. Imagine you were taking a trip to Denver, Colorado, and needed directions to get somewhere in the city. If you had a friend who had been "near Denver" who wanted to give you directions, would you trust his NDE (near-Denver experience), or would you rather turn to a safer, more accurate guide composed by someone who had actually been to Denver?[10] Would you rather have the near-Denver directions to your final destination or follow an official map of the city? Or even better yet, you could get your information directly from someone who had been to Denver.

For anyone who wants to know more about the afterlife, I would urge you to stay away from books by people claiming to know firsthand what lies behind the veil of death. Instead, read God's official map to your final destination in His Word.

Jesus has been to the other side and back. He is the only One who is qualified to tell us what lies behind earthly life. To the apostle John, Jesus said, "'Do not be afraid; I am the first and the last, and the living One; and I was dead, and behold, I am alive forevermore, and I have the keys of death and, of Hades'" (Revelation 1:17–18).

He knows the way. He is THE way. Follow Him.

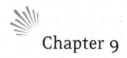

Chapter 9

DO SOME PEOPLE GET A GLIMPSE OF HEAVEN BEFORE THEY DIE?

There is another experience related to death and dying that many people have wondered about through the centuries. Very near the moment of their passing, some people seem to catch a glimpse of where they are heading and are able to speak a few words about it.

These occurrences are commonly called deathbed visions (DBV), sometimes referred to as "first cousins" of near-death experiences. The key difference is that with deathbed visions the person actually dies not long after the experience, while near-death experience are just that—near death.

According to studies, only about 10 percent of patients are conscious at or just before the moment of death. But of those 10 percent, about half appear to have some kind of deathbed visions. People often claim to see deceased loved ones, religious or biblical figures, or heaven itself, and to show surprising mood changes.[11]

Unlike NDEs, there is a biblical basis and evidence for believing in the reality of DBVs. In Acts 7, the great Spirit-filled saint named Stephen was stoned to death in Jerusalem by the religious leaders for his faith in Jesus as Messiah and Lord. As the stones fell and death closed in, this good man very clearly saw something no one else in that crowd could see.

> But being full of the Holy Spirit, he gazed intently into heaven and saw the glory of God, and Jesus standing at the right hand of God; and he said, "Behold, I see the heavens opened up and the Son of Man standing at the right hand of God." (vv. 55–56)

In every other place where the Bible mentions Jesus being at the Father's right hand, He is always seated. But here Jesus is standing. Why? To show His compassionate concern for this first martyr of the church and to welcome His faithful servant to heaven.

D. L. Moody's story does not appear in the pages of Scripture. Yet the documented account of this great evangelist's deathbed vision is yet one more affirmation of this possibility for believers.[12]

In August 1899 in New York City, four months before he died, Moody made this triumphant statement:

> Someday you will read in the papers that Dwight Moody is dead. Don't you believe a word of it! At that moment I shall be more alive than I am now.... I was

born of the flesh in 1837; I was born of the Spirit in 1855. That which is born of the flesh may die. That which is born of the Spirit shall live forever.

Four months later, on December 22, Moody lay dying. Early in the morning, his son Will was startled by his father's voice from the bed across the room. "Earth recedes, heaven opens before me!" Will hurried to his father's side, and Moody said, "This is no dream, Will. It is beautiful.... If this is death, it is sweet. There is no valley here. God is calling me and I must go. Don't call me back!" The great evangelist then slipped back into what appeared to be unconsciousness.

A few hours later Moody revived to find his wife and family gathered around him. He said to his wife, "I went to the gate of heaven. Why, it is so wonderful, and I saw the children [Irene and Dwight, who had died in childhood]."

After a short time elapsed, Moody spoke again, "This is my triumph! This is my coronation day! It is glorious." After that the man who stirred two nations for Christ drew his final breath of air on this earth and entered the gate of heaven.

Billy Graham records a similar account of his grandmother's death. He says:

> When my maternal grandmother died...the room seemed to fill with a heavenly light. She sat up in bed and almost laughingly said, "I see Jesus. He has His arms out-stretched toward me. I see Ben [her husband, who had died some years earlier] and I see the angels." She slumped over, absent from the body but present with the Lord.[13]

What are we to make of such accounts? Were these deathbed visions real or imagined? I guess there's no way to prove absolutely either way for sure. But we can say from Stephen's experience that this sort of experience is biblical. We know that it happened at least once in the Bible. Personally, I have no reason to doubt the reality of such accounts.

It's important for us to remember, however, that we don't *need* these kinds of visions and experiences—comforting as they might be—to convince us of the reality of heaven. Our belief in heaven is based on God's promises in His Word. Nor should we expect this sort of experience to happen in every case…but it certainly could. God is sovereign. He acts according to His own purposes, not in some formulaic fashion. There is only one instance of this in the Bible. By this lone occurrence, God may be trying to tell us not to expect it as common—but also not to totally discount it either.

If God in His grace and mercy chooses to grant some of His children an early glimpse of glory just before death, as he did for Stephen, D. L. Moody, and Billy Graham's grandmother, we should accept it and thank Him for it as another demonstration of His matchless grace.

How wonderful it would be if we should live in such a way that the Son of God Himself would stand up to welcome us to glory.

Chapter 10

IS REINCARNATION CONSISTENT WITH THE BIBLE?

The Bible clearly teaches life after death. But the idea known as reincarnation teaches life after life…after life…after life…until one ultimately attains some state of nirvana or eternal nothingness.

It's difficult to give a concrete definition of reincarnation since there are various models of what it really entails. The word *reincarnation* means "rebirth in another body." The basic thread that runs through all the definitions of this belief is the notion that after death the soul or life force passes into another body before its birth. The goal of this process is a kind of spiritual evolution.[14]

Reincarnation is the world view of Buddhists, Hindus, Sikhs, Krishna, Bahai, and Jains.

But surprisingly, according to a Gallup poll, 25 percent of Americans say they believe in reincarnation.[15] Another 20 percent were not sure if they believed in reincarnation. Even many professing Christians have no problem embracing reincarnation, believing that it can somehow be harmonized with the teachings of the Bible.

Support for reincarnation is primarily drawn from human experience—the concept of déjà vu or remembering details from a past life. Of course, this hardly serves as solid proof. Some people actually point to specific Scriptures to support reincarnation. Here are the verses they often use:

"Before I formed you in the womb I knew you, and before you were born I consecrated you; I have appointed you a prophet to the nations." (Jeremiah 1:5)

All this verse is saying is that the eternal God ordained Jeremiah to his prophetic office before he was even born.

As He passed by, He saw a man blind from birth. And His disciples asked Him, "Rabbi, who sinned, this man or his parents, that he would be born blind?" (John 9:1–2)

Those who use this verse maintain that it reflects a belief by the disciples of paying off karmic debt for himself and his parents.[16] *In the very next verse,* however, Jesus totally dispels any false notion that the man was paying for sins.

Jesus answered, "It was neither that this man sinned, nor his parents; but it was so that the works of God might be displayed in him." (John 9:3)

In another New Testament passage, advocates of reincarnation latch onto Jesus' words concerning John the Baptist:

"And if you are willing to accept it, John himself is Elijah who was to come." (Matthew 11:14)

Was Jesus saying that John the Baptist was Elijah reincarnated? In fact, John himself refutes such a notion. When asked flat-out if he was Elijah, John said, "'I am not'" (John 1:21). John came in the power and spirit of Elijah; that is, with an Elijah-like ministry. But John and Elijah were two separate persons.

The other main model of the afterlife, besides reincarnation, is resurrection. *Resurrection* literally means "restoration in our present bodies." As you can see from the definitions themselves, reincarnation and resurrection are vastly different. Actually, they are mutually exclusive.

Reincarnation means "rebirth in another body."

Resurrection means "restoration in our present bodies."

Both can't be true.

So which is right? What does the Bible say? There are at least seven biblical arguments in favor of resurrection and against reincarnation.

First, the Greek word *anastasis,* which is translated "resurrection" in our English translations, occurs forty-two times in the New Testament. The verb *anisteemi* ("to raise or raise up") is used with reference to the raising of dead bodies numerous times in the New Testament, especially the "raising up" of Jesus from the dead on the third day. The word *reincarnation* or similar words are not found in the New Testament. Resurrection is a biblical term. Reincarnation is not.

Second, the Bible teaches one death for each person. "And inasmuch as it is appointed for men to die once and after this comes judgment" (Hebrews 9:27). Or, as Eugene Peterson paraphrased the verse in *The Message,* "Everyone has to die once, then face the consequences."

Third, as we have already seen in earlier chapters, the Bible teaches that at death the soul goes immediately to either heaven or hades, not into another body (Luke 16:19–31).

Fourth, the Bible says that our hope is the "redemption of our [bodies]" (Romans 8:23), not the reincarnation of our soul into a series of bodies—one after another.

Fifth, the resurrection of Jesus is a historical fact. We know from history and the Bible that Jesus was raised from the dead. And His resurrection is the foundation for the resurrection of our bodies (1 Corinthians 15:20). Reincarnation, on the other hand, is based on human speculation, myth, and fantasy.

Sixth, the Bible teaches the *transformation* of our present bodies, while reincarnation teaches the *transmigration* of souls from one body to another.[17]

For our citizenship is in heaven, from which also we eagerly wait for a Savior, the Lord Jesus Christ; who will *transform* the body of our humble state into conformity with the body of His glory, by the exertion of the power He has even to subject all things to Himself. (Philippians 3:20–21)

In the Bible, the same body that dies is resurrected. And while it will be vastly different from the body we have now, there is a continuity with our present body. "So also is the resurrection of the dead. It is sown a perishable body, it is raised an imperishable body; it is sown in dishonor, it is raised in glory; it is sown in weakness, it is raised in power; it is sown a natural body, it is raised a spiritual body" (1 Corinthians 15:42–44a).

Seventh, the Bible teaches that through the atoning work of Christ on the cross, man can be forgiven of all his sins by simply trusting in Jesus and His once-for-all death and resurrection. Belief in resurrection is a key element in the saving gospel of Christ (1 Corinthians 15:1–3). Reincarnation teaches the concept of karma, which means that evil deeds in past lives have implications for this present life. It teaches self-salvation. Ultimate liberation, achieved by man himself, is release from the cyclical wheel of rebirth. God's Word says that man is fallen and can only find salvation, hope, and release from sin by God's grace and forgiveness through Jesus Christ alone (John 14:6; Ephesians 1:7).

As you can see, these two worldviews could not be more different. Reincarnation is mystical and man-centered. Resurrection is grounded in historical fact and the Scriptures and is God-centered.

Chapter 11

CAN THE DEAD COMMUNICATE WITH THE LIVING?

According to a recent Gallup poll, 38 percent of Americans believe that ghosts or spirits can come back in certain situations and communicate with the living. (This is up from 25 percent in 1990.) Another 17 percent weren't sure.[18] The same poll also revealed that 28 percent of Americans believe that some people can hear from or talk to dead people. (This is up from 18 percent in 1990.) Another 26 percent weren't sure.

In the 1999 movie *The Sixth Sense,* a boy communicates with spirits that don't know they're dead. In the movie, the boy utters that now famous line "I see dead people." Apparently a lot of people believe that we can see or at least hear from dead people. The number of Americans who believe some people can hear from or talk to dead people is a staggering 80 million. That's quite a market. Spiritism and alleged communication with the dead has now gone mainstream in America.

John Edward is a psychic who has made headlines on television by "helping people communicate with the dead." Edward has appeared on the *Oprah Winfrey Show*, *Larry King Live*, and *20/20*. But unlike the spiritualists of days gone by, who typically plied their trade in darkroom séances, Edward and his ilk often perform before live audiences and on national television. Edward has his own popular show on the SciFi channel and CBS2 called *Crossing Over*, which has gone into national syndication.

Before we answer the questions concerning communication with the dead, it's important that we know what we're discussing. Here are a few helpful definitions.

Medium: "An individual held to be a channel of communication between the earthly world and a world of spirits."[19] An intermediary between spirits and people.

Spiritist: A person who believes in spiritism, the existence and manifestation of spirits.

Psychic: "A person apparently sensitive to nonphysical forces."[20]

Necromancy: "Conjuration of the spirits of the dead for purposes of magically revealing the future or influencing the course of events."[21]

FORBIDDEN TERRITORY

The first thing we need to know about the idea of contacting or communicating with the dead is that the Bible explicitly forbids it.

"There shall not be found among you anyone...who uses divination, one who practices witchcraft, or one who interprets omens, or a sorcerer, or one who casts a spell, or a medium, or a spiritist, or one who calls up the dead. For whoever does these things is detestable to the

LORD; and because of these detestable things the LORD your God will drive them out before you. You shall be blameless before the LORD your God." (Deuteronomy 18:10–13)

"Do not turn to mediums or spiritists; do not seek them out to be defiled by them. I am the LORD your God." (Leviticus 19:31)

"As for the person who turns to mediums and to spiritists, to play the harlot after them, I will also set My face against that person and will cut him off from among his people. Now a man or a woman who is a medium or a spiritist shall surely be put to death. They shall be stoned with stones, their bloodguiltiness is upon them." (Leviticus 20:6, 27)

God Himself wanted to reveal what His people needed to know through His prophets (Deuteronomy 18:9–22). We have this revelation today in our Bible and through the illuminating ministry and guidance of His Holy Spirit. We need no other source of guidance about things, visible or invisible.

SOMETIMES IT APPEARS TO WORK

Second, mediums, spiritists, and necromancers do often tell people things about their departed loved ones that seem amazingly accurate. How do we explain this? Sometimes, of course, it may be nothing more than an insightful medium or spiritist who knows how to look for clues from someone seeking information. Those who practice spiritism are often very gifted in their ability to do what's referred to as "cold calling" or "cold reading." They also use other methods known as "warm reading" and "hot reading."

Michael Gleghorn, a research associate for Probe ministries, gives this description of these various techniques modern psychics and mediums employ:

> In cold reading, mediums make use of methods that help them "read" a person who was unknown to them in advance. Such methods may include observing body language, asking questions, and inviting the subject to interpret vague statements. For instance, by carefully observing body language and facial expressions, the medium can often get a good idea of whether or not he's on the right track. Also, by asking questions and inviting the subject to interpret vague statements, the medium can gain valuable information. This information can then be used later in the reading to make what appear to be stunningly precise revelations from the spirit world.... Warm reading involves making statements that tend to apply to most anyone. For example, many people carry a piece of jewelry that belonged to their dead loved one. By asking if the subject is carrying such jewelry, the medium has a good chance of making a "hit." This can give the impression that the information was divined from a paranormal source. In reality, of course, it may have been nothing more than a highly probable guess.... The last technique, hot reading, actually involves getting information about a subject *before* the reading begins![22]

While these techniques are the most common explanation for how these modern mediums ply their trade, there may be another more sinister explanation. It's also possible that these modern-day mediums may at times have a pipeline into the unseen spirit world via demonic spirits. The main work of Satan and his minions is deception. What better way to deceive the unsuspecting than to wow them with information from the great beyond! The information given by mediums and spiritists is always contradictory to Scripture.

Michael Gleghorn notes:

In addition, listen to what the spirits are alleged to say. Do any of them, like the rich man, strive to warn their relatives about a place of conscious torment? Do they urge repentance for sin or the need for personal faith in Christ? On the contrary, such important Christian doctrines are typically either ignored or denied. But if the Bible is truly God's Word, and the spirits deny its teachings, then who are these spirits likely to be?[23]

Make no mistake. No matter how you slice it, this is nothing to mess around with.

What About 1 Samuel 28?

There is at least one example in the Bible of communication with the dead. It's found in 1 Samuel 28, one of the most fascinating chapters in all the Bible. It's the story of King Saul's surprising séance with a female medium in the town of En-dor. Saul was preparing for a battle against the Philistines on Mt. Gilboa. He prayed to the Lord for guidance, but the Lord refused to hear him. Since Saul had refused to listen to God, God now refused to listen to Saul.

In desperation, the tormented king sought out a well-known medium for information about the future. Since Saul knew that the witch would refuse to cooperate with him if she knew who he was, he disguised himself. After lying to the woman by swearing to her that God would not punish her for breaking God's law, Saul asked her to bring up the spirit of the prophet Samuel from Sheol. And to the utter shock of the woman it actually worked! Samuel really appeared. This shows that the woman had never actually been successful in doing this before. She was more shocked than Saul.

Some have maintained that what came up was actually a demon who impersonated Samuel. But the message that followed was clearly from God.

So how do we explain this event in view of God's commands not to engage in necromancy or conjuring up of spirits? Why did God allow this? Clearly, in this one case God permitted the conjuring up of a spirit. God apparently allowed this as a further judgment on Saul. God sent Samuel to give Saul a prophetic message—a word of judgment. Samuel's message was that Saul and his son Jonathan would fall in battle the next day at the hands of the Philistines and join him in the afterlife. Filled with fear when he heard these words, Saul fell flat on the ground. The next day, God's Word through Samuel was completely and tragically fulfilled.

This passage, rather than condoning contacting the dead, further substantiates God's prohibition against consulting mediums or spiritists. The only message God had for Saul was judgment. So, while this incident proves that communication with the dead is *possible,* the fact that it's the only such instance of this in the Bible also shows that it's not *probable.* The rich man in Luke 16 wanted God to send Lazarus back to communicate the need for repentance to his five brothers who were still alive. If the dead are able to communicate with the living, why didn't the rich man just tell them himself? The reason is obvious—he was unable to do so.

Also, have you ever noticed that every medium and spiritist

always has *positive* messages from those on the other side? Everything is always sunshine and flowers. But in the only biblical case of communicating with the dead, the message was anything but positive. God told Saul he was a dead man.

When it comes to the subject of revelation, we must remember that God has given us His Word as a lamp to our feet and a light to our path (Psalm 119:105). Turning to other sources of alleged revelation is taking a blind leap in the dark.

Chapter 12

IS FEAR OF DEATH NORMAL?

I heard a story recently about a Catholic priest, a Protestant minister, and a Jewish rabbi who were discussing what they would like people to say after they died and their bodies were on display in open caskets.

The Catholic priest said, "I would like someone to say, 'He was a righteous man, an honest man, and very generous.'"

The Protestant minister said, "I would like someone to say, 'He was very kind and fair, and he was very good to his parishioners.'"

The Jewish rabbi said, "I would like someone to say, 'Oh look! He's moving!'"

This humorous story reveals the way most people think about death. It's something they want to avoid at all costs. It scares them, so they want to avoid it—or even thinking about it. As Woody Allen once said, "It's not that I'm afraid to die. I just don't want to be there when it happens."

When you think about it, death is always pictured as a dark, frightening, shadowy figure with a sharp sickle in hand. The

Grim Reaper. The Bible speaks forthrightly of this fear of death. It says that those who don't know the Lord are enslaved to the fear of death all their lives (Hebrews 2:15). Death is the king of terrors. It's the ultimate fear known to mankind. And it's no respecter of persons. It comes to all. Rich and poor. Famous and unknown. Wise and foolish.

After several heart surgeries, interviewer Larry King has done quite a bit of thinking about the afterlife. His recent comments probably express the view of many people. "Right now my opinion is, I hope there's an afterlife, but I think this is it. That's why I fear death. Religious people never fear death, only the sadness of losing someone. If I knew that I was going to go to a place that's better than this, why wouldn't I want to go now? That has always confounded me."[24]

Even believers are not exempt from this fear. In the Old Testament, Hezekiah, a godly king of Judah, faced a life-and-death struggle (2 Kings 20:1–11). He was extremely ill and was informed by the prophet Isaiah that he would die. Grief-stricken by the news, the king prayed to God with bitter weeping. Hezekiah had no desire to die. His actions seem to betray a lurking fear of death. In response to his cry, the Lord granted Hezekiah a fifteen-year extension of life.

Perhaps you can identify with Hezekiah today. All of us at one time or another have faced the nagging anxiety or fear of death when we had some undiagnosed pain or illness. We've agonized over the prospect of death for a loved one.

Why do we have this fear? Is there a way to get rid of it once and for all?

CAUSE OF THE FEAR OF DEATH

The fear of death undoubtedly has many causes. But there are three that stand out.

One reason people fear death is simply apprehension of the unknown. While the Bible does tell us some things about the afterlife, most of it remains a mystery. This unknown aspect can leave us asking all kinds of what-if questions. Or maybe you sometimes even wonder if it's all true. Nagging doubts can lead to a paralyzing fear of death.

A second cause of fearing death is the prospect of accountability or standing before God. This, I believe, is the real issue lurking behind most fear of death. Deep down inside, people know they have sinned and have a sense that they will be held accountable for what they have done. Even believers can worry about standing before the judgment seat of Christ. This latter worry, however, is unfounded since the issue at the judgment seat of Christ will *not* be our eternal destiny, but rewards or lack of rewards based on how we have lived our life as a believer.

A third reason people fear death is because the whole idea of eternity—living *forever*—is beyond our finite minds. Something so far beyond our ability to grasp can fill our hearts with a sense of dread or feeling overwhelmed. Ecclesiastes 3:11 says that God has set eternity in the heart of every person, but even so, thinking about eternity and living forever will certainly overwhelm us if we dwell on it too long. The finite must openly recognize its frailty and fear in the face of the infinite. Eternity is simply too big for us.

VICTORY OVER DEATH

God's remedy for the fear of death is simple, yet very profound. The Bible teaches that Jesus came to release us forever from the fear of death. Hebrews 2:14–15 says, "Since the children share in flesh and blood, He Himself likewise also partook of the same, that through death He might render powerless him who had the power of death, that is, the devil; and might free those who through fear of death were subject to slavery all their lives."

Christ came in human flesh, died for us, and through His resurrection conquered Satan who had the power of death. No believer in Jesus Christ should ever allow the enemy to torment him or her with the paralyzing anxiety of what-ifs about death. Jesus experienced death for us and conquered it. We must take hold of this truth by faith and receive Christ's peace in the face of death. Faith in God's promises is the antidote to fear. Christ's conquest of death even provides comfort from fear at the loss of a loved one. Believers grieve, yes, but not as those who have no hope (1 Thessalonians 4:13–18).

When contemplating the prospect of his own death, the apostle Paul said that to die was gain and that departing to be with Christ was "very much better" than life here on earth (Philippians 1:21–23). For the Christian, death brings a better inheritance, a better fellowship, and a better body. While it's difficult for us to imagine heaven, it will be incomparably, infinitely better than life here on earth. There's nothing to fear.

THE STING OF DEATH

For the believer death has lost its victory. Yes, death is still an enemy. Our final enemy. But Christ has removed its sting! "Death is swallowed up in victory. O death, where is your victory? O death, where is your sting?" (1 Corinthians 15:54b–55).

One spring day a little boy was riding in the car with his dad when a bee came flying in the window. The little boy heard the buzzing sound and was scared to death. He began to scream, "Dad, *do* something! The bee is going to sting me!" The dad reached out his hand, grabbed the bee, held it in his hand for a few seconds and then released it.

The bee began to fly and buzz around the car again, and the boy was frightened again. But the father said, "Son, you don't have to be afraid anymore. All the bee can do now is make noise." The dad then held out his hand and showed his son the stinger in the palm of his hand.

On the cross, for you and for me, Jesus took the stinger of sin, which is death. So all that death can do now for those who have trusted in Jesus Christ is buzz around and make a lot of noise.[25]

The Shadow of Death

Donald Grey Barnhouse, the famous pastor of Tenth Presbyterian Church in Philadelphia, told a powerful story to illustrate the prospect of death for a believer. Barnhouse had just attended the funeral of his wife and was driving his young children home. Driving along, he kept trying to think of some way to explain their mother's death to them, so they could understand. About that time, while sitting at a red light, a semitrailer crossed in front of them in the intersection, momentarily engulfing the car in its shadow. Turning to his children, Barnhouse asked, "Would you rather have been struck by that truck or its shadow?"

"The shadow, of course," they replied.

Barnhouse paused for a moment to reflect, and said, "That's what happens to Christians when we die. Jesus was hit by the truck of death head-on so those who trust in Him are only hit by the shadow. Those who don't know Him are hit by the full force of death."[26]

Because of what Christ accomplished for us on the cross by dying in our place, death no longer carries the pain and fear it once did. That's the truth of the gospel. Jesus died in your place and rose triumphantly from the grave. He took the full force of the semi of death head-on, so all that's left for you and me is the shadow.

Receive Jesus Christ as your Savior from sin.

Forever is a long time. Don't miss heaven. Don't miss Christ.

Remove any doubt or fear about where you will spend eternity. Invite Jesus into your life today!

PART TWO

Grave
Matters

Chapter 13

SHOULD CHRISTIANS BE CREMATED?

One question that always comes up when discussing issues related to death and the afterlife is the method of dealing with the body after death. More and more people are wondering whether it's acceptable for Christians to be cremated. Is it a biblical practice? How might it affect our bodily existence in the next life?

THE CREMATION CRAZE

Historically, there are three ways of handling bodies. First, the ancient Egyptians practiced mummification in an attempt to preserve the body indefinitely. Second, the Greeks and Romans—who held a strongly dualistic view and believed all matter was evil—practiced cremation. Hindus, who believe in reincarnation, also dispose of bodies by cremation. Third, Jews and Christians practiced burial.

Today, there are really two mains options available for the

disposal of bodies: burning or burial. And while burial is still the majority practice, cremation is gaining ground quickly (no pun intended) in the United States and Canada. Consider these statistics:

Year:	1962	1992	1996	2000	2010
Unites States	5%	20%		25%	40% (estimated)
Canada			36%		50% (estimated)

A few years ago, a polling organization found that those who intend to choose cremation for themselves or their loved ones has increased to 46 percent, up from 32 percent in 1990. By the year 2010, it is estimated that 65 percent of people in New England states will choose cremation for the disposal of their physical remains.[27]

WHY CHOOSE CREMATION?

There are undoubtedly many reasons why people choose cremation. I believe three major reasons stand out. First, there is an *emotional* reason. Some people believe that cremation brings immediate closure to the grieving process. And because our contemporary society is so mobile, the idea of family burial plots has less and less appeal as the years go by. Without this tie to family and the past, cremation is an easier decision emotionally.

Second, there is an *ecological* reason. Simply stated, cremation doesn't waste valuable land that could be used for more productive purposes. In Japan, where land is so valuable, burial is sometimes illegal, and the cremation rate is 98 percent. But how big a problem is the land issue in North America? While there may be some areas of the U.S. and Canada where this is a legitimate problem, in the majority of places, there is land to spare for cemeteries.

Third, the primary reason given is usually *economical.* Cremation is less expensive. Much less expensive in some cases. I do find it interesting, however, that people with higher incomes are more likely to choose cremation than those with lower incomes.

As a pastor, I have noticed a dramatic increase in cremations in the funerals I have performed in the last few years. All of this raises the question in many people's minds: Should Christians be cremated? Is it unscriptural for a Christian to make such a choice?

BURIAL AND THE BIBLE

There are three examples of cremation in the Old Testament.

1. Achan (Joshua 7:25).
2. Saul (1 Samuel 31:12). (Saul was probably cremated because his body had already partially decomposed and to prevent further desecration of the body by the Philistines. But notice that his bones were buried.)
3. The King of Edom (Amos 2:1).

Interestingly, each of these instances involves God's judgment or curse in some way. That should tell us something. Even so, we must say that the Bible never *explicitly* condemns cremation.

Nevertheless, I believe there are eight solid scriptural reasons for a Christian to choose burial, if at all possible, as the means of disposing of his or her body.

First, Scripture clearly favors burial over cremation in both the Old and New Testaments. Believers are always buried in the Bible. Beginning all the way back in Genesis, burial is presented as the biblical practice. Here are just a few illustrations:

- Abraham (Genesis 15:15).
- Sarah (Genesis 23:4–6).
- John the Baptist (Mark 6:29).
- Ananias and Sapphira (Acts 5:6–10).
- Stephen (Acts 8:2).

Second, when Moses died, God buried his body. Deuteronomy 34:5–6 says, "So Moses the servant of the LORD died there in the land of Moab, according to the word of the LORD. And He buried him in the valley in the land of Moab, opposite Beth-peor; but no man knows his burial place to this day."

Evidently, God buried Moses in an undisclosed place so the people wouldn't be tempted to turn his burial site into a shrine and fall into false worship as they were so prone to do (see Jude 1:9). To accomplish this purpose, God could have instantly burned his body to settle the problem once and for all. But He didn't. The fact that God practiced burial with the body of Moses should speak to us today concerning God's preference for the disposal of bodies.

Third, in the Incarnation, when the Word (Jesus) became flesh, God uniquely sanctified human life and bodily existence forever.

Fourth, burial highlights the sanctity of the human body as created by God in His image (Genesis 1:27; 1 Corinthians 6:13, 19–20).

Fifth, as we have already seen, burning bodies frequently carries the idea of judgment or a curse. At the conclusion of the Nuremberg War Trials, the bodies of the war criminals were cremated and their ashes were scattered in an undisclosed place. The imagery behind this act was judgment, disdain, and humiliation. In biblical Judaism, only the bodies of criminals were burned. Their bodies were thrown into the Hinnom Valley (the city dump) outside the city of Jerusalem. Jesus used this smoldering valley as a picture of hell. As Dr. Norman Geisler notes, "The Christian has escaped the judgment of fire presented in the Bible (Revelation 20:14). Cremation is the wrong picture to remind believers of *salvation in the body* by resurrection."[28]

Sixth, Christian tradition clearly favors burial as a symbol of the promise of future resurrection. As the catacombs in Rome disclose, the early Christians insisted on burying their dead. Christian gravesites were called *koimeteria* (cemeteries) which literally means "sleeping places." This reflected the Christian belief in the future resurrection of the body.[29] According to 1 Corinthians 15:36–37, 42–22, putting the body in the ground is like sowing a seed. Burial is consistent with the Christian concept of resurrection.

Seventh, Jesus was buried, and our baptism is equated with both burial and resurrection (Romans 6:4). Remember, Joseph of Arimathea went to great personal expense to bury the body of the Lord Jesus.

Eighth, burial best communicates what we believe. The first known cremation in America did not occur until 1876—accompanied by readings from Charles Darwin and ancient Hindu writings. For many years after that time, most of the people cremated in America were liberals and freethinkers. Their choice in the disposal of their bodies was consistent with their beliefs. It communicated something.

As believers in Jesus Christ, the real question we need to ask about this issue is what are we communicating to our families, friends, and community about our beliefs by our choice to be buried or cremated? As followers of Christ, we should act in life and death in ways that are consistent with what we believe and communicate what we believe to a watching world. We don't want to do anything to blunt the reality of death or the glorious truth of bodily resurrection. I believe that burial, as opposed to cremation, is the best way to communicate to others our belief in creation, incarnation, and resurrection.

THE DEAD WILL BE RAISED

Having said all this, we must recognize that cremation is not an issue affecting salvation in any way. Nor is it an issue of God's power. Cremation poses no difficulty for God. God has no problem resurrecting a body, cremated or otherwise. Philippians 3:21 tells us that God, who has the power to subject all things to Himself, can transform our bodies into conformity with Christ's glorious resurrection body. There is plenty of power.

In fact, God will raise the bodies of those who have been burned to death, who have died in violent explosions, or who have been eaten by wild animals. He knows the location of every atom. And at the Rapture, He will resurrect the bodies of every one of His children, regardless of where their body is or what happened to it after death. "The dead will be raised imperishable" (1 Corinthians 15:52).

There are no exceptions!

The real issue at stake here is what best communicates what we believe—our worldview. And I believe that burial accomplishes this goal while cremation does not.

PART THREE

The Other Side of the Good News

Chapter 14

IS HELL
A REAL PLACE?

A headline in a newspaper a few years ago must have caused a few people to choke on their coffee. It read "It May Be Harder to Get to Hell This Year."

It may be harder to get to Hell this year. A bridge on the main road leading to Hell, Michigan, is badly in need of repair, a project that could close the road for three months. Business owners in the town fear that the disruption in traffic would force some stores into bankruptcy. "It'll close the whole town," complained Jim Lee, the president of the Hell Chamber of Commerce. Officials acknowledged that the repair work will cause some disruption but insist that the plans to fix the road to Hell are paved with good intentions. The road has suffered great damage each time Hell freezes over.[30]

Sadly, it's all too easy to get to the real place called hell in the Bible. All you have to do is…nothing at all. Most people ignore the warnings. They choose to simply wish it all away. Unbelievers often reject the idea of hell altogether, while many believers ignore it. But surprisingly, belief in a literal hell is on the rise, according to some recent polls.

USA Today often publishes statistics that shape the nation on the front page of the paper. A few years ago, the editors presented interesting statistics on how people answered the question, "Is there a hell?" According to these results, 52 percent of adults are certain there's a hell, and 27 percent think there might be.

Conducting a similar poll, the Gallup organization found that 70 percent of Americans now believe in hell. This is up from 56 percent just since 1997.[31] Clearly, hell is making a sobering comeback.

The Bible clearly teaches a literal place called "hell." In the parable of the rich man and Lazarus in Luke 16:19–31, hell, or hades, is pictured as a literal place where the unrighteous rich man immediately went when he died. The man is pictured as being conscious, having awareness of his surroundings, and fully remembering his life on earth.

It may surprise many people to know that eleven of the twelve times the word *gehenna* (hell) occurs in the New Testament, it is found on the lips of the Savior Himself. Make no mistake, Jesus believed in a literal place called hell. He talked about it more than any other person in the Bible. And He talked about hell more than He talked about heaven.

In His famous Sermon on the Mount, Jesus mentioned hell or final judgment at least six times. In His Olivet Discourse, two days before His death on the cross, Jesus spoke of final judgment numerous times. The final verse of this great sermon says, "These will go away into eternal punishment, but the righteous into eternal life" (Matthew 25:46). Jesus affirmed the existence of both hell and heaven in this one sentence. You can't believe in one without the other.

Jesus is our primary source for the existence of a real place called hell and the descriptions of what hell is like.

Chapter 15

WHAT IS
HELL LIKE?

I n a recent *USA Today* poll, pollsters first asked respondents if they believed in the existence of hell. They followed up with the question, "What do you think hell will be like?"

The answers were interesting.

- 48 percent believe it is a real place where people suffer eternal torment.
- 46 percent say it is an anguished state of existence rather than an actual place.
- 6 percent don't know.

U.S. News and World Report, in an article titled "Hell Hath No Fury," provided this information from a survey titled "What Comes Closest to Your Idea of Hell?" Here are the results:

- 34 percent believe hell is a real place where people suffer eternal fiery torments.
- 53 percent believe hell is an anguished state of existence eternally separated from God.
- 11 percent don't know.

In yet another survey, this time from the Barna organization, people revealed their ideas of what hell is like.[32]

- 39 percent believe hell is a state of eternal separation from God's presence.
- 32 percent say it's an actual place of torment and suffering where people's souls go after death.
- 13 percent believe hell is just symbolic of an unknown bad outcome after death.
- 16 percent weren't sure or said they didn't believe in an afterlife.

Most people in America believe in a place called hell, but ideas about what it is are far from unanimous. Many have concocted their own theories about hell. Someone once said, "Hell is Manhattan at rush hour." [33]

While people might joke about hell, make light of it, and come up with their own theories about whether it even exists at all, the Bible gives us God's terrifying view of hell. And it is no joking matter. The Bible never gives us a complete, detailed description of what hell is like, but it does provide us with several frightening, sobering facts about hell.

Here are ten terrible facts about hell from the pages of the Bible. These are biblical truths that should convince any sane person that he or she would never, never want to end up there.

Fact #1: Hell was NOT originally created for human beings.

In Matthew 25:41, Jesus reveals a very important truth about hell: "Then He will also say to those on His left, 'Depart from Me, accursed ones, into the eternal fire which has been prepared for the devil and his angels.'"

Nevertheless, those who make the same tragic decision as Satan will suffer the same fate.

Fact #2: Hell is a place of memory.

In hell there will be continued consciousness and immediate awareness of where one is. In Luke 16:19–31, the rich man knew immediately *where he was*.

There will also be identity—the rich man knew *who he was*.

There will also be memory. When the rich man asked Abraham for some water to cool the burning of his tongue, he answered, "Child, remember that during your life you received your good things" (v. 25).

We also know from Jesus that the rich man remembered Lazarus (Luke 16:24) and his five brothers who were still alive (vv. 27–28). People in hell will have perfect memories and will suffer the mental and emotional anguish of regret.

Fact #3: Hell is a place of conscious physical, mental, and spiritual torment.

The worst part of hell is that there will be torment and agony. The rich man said, "I am in agony in this flame" (Luke 16:24). He described hades as "this place of torment" (v. 28).

Fact #4: Hell is a place of unquenchable fire.

"The Son of Man will send forth His angels, and they will gather out of His kingdom all stumbling blocks, and those who commit lawlessness, and will throw them into the furnace of fire; in that place there will be weeping and gnashing of teeth." (Matthew 13:41–42)

"It is better for you to enter the kingdom of God with one eye, than, having two eyes, to be cast into hell, where their worm does not die, and the fire is not quenched. For everyone will be salted with fire." (Mark 9:47–49)

"I am in agony in this flame." (Luke 16:24)

Fact #5: Hell is a place of separation from God.

These will pay the penalty of eternal destruction, away from the presence of the Lord and from the glory of His power. (2 Thessalonians 1:9)

Fact #6: Hell is a place of unspeakable misery, sorrow, anger, and frustration.

"There will be weeping and gnashing of teeth." (Matthew 13:42)

Fact #7: Hell is a place of unsatisfied, raging thirst.

"And he cried out and said, 'Father Abraham, have mercy on me, and send Lazarus so that he may dip the tip of his finger in water and cool off my tongue.'" (Luke 16:24)

Fact #8: Hell is the only other place to spend eternity besides heaven.

In other words, there are only two places people go after death—paradise or perdition. As we have already seen earlier in this book, there is no in-between place. There is no third choice. The rich man went to hades; Lazarus went to paradise. These are still the only two options today.

Fact #9: Hell is a place where the inhabitants don't want others to come.

The rich man in Luke 16 never complains that it is unfair for him to be there. He sadly bemoans his torment, but never says he is there unjustly. However, he longs to get word to his brothers who are still alive of what they must do to avoid his fate. He has compassion for his five living brothers and knows that for his brothers to escape hades, they must repent (v. 30).

The rich man in hades suddenly became interested in evangelism and missions! As Erwin Lutzer poignantly says,

> We might think this man would have preferred to have his brothers join him in hades for the sake of the companionship. But he was more than willing to never see them again if he only knew that they would be on the other side of the gulf where Lazarus and Abraham were meeting for the first time. Apparently, even in hades there is compassion, a natural human concern about the fate of those who are loved.[34]

Fact #10: Hell is earned.

Hell is what we earn. "For the wages of sin is death" (Romans 6:23a). Heaven is what God gives us as a free gift by His grace. "But the free gift of God is eternal life in Christ Jesus our Lord" (v. 23b).

Our admission price to heaven was paid in full by the blood of Jesus Christ. Make sure you have accepted it before it's too late.

Chapter 16

ARE THERE DIFFERENT PARTS OF THE UNDERWORLD?

When we talk about the underworld or netherworld, the word that we usually employ is *hell*. *Webster's New Collegiate Dictionary* defines hell as "a nether world in which the dead continue to exist; the nether realm of the devil and the demons in which the damned suffer everlasting punishment." Hell is kind of the catchall word we use for the abode of the devil, demons, and damned humans.

The Bible itself, however, is much more specific and precise in its description of the nether realm than most people realize. According to the Bible, the underworld is divided into different parts. The first hints of this are found in the Old Testament. "For a fire is kindled in My anger, and burns to *the lowest part* of Sheol, and consumes the earth with its yield, and sets on fire the foundations of the mountains" (Deuteronomy 32:22).

In the Old Testament the word *Sheol* is the general term for the place of the departed dead. It can mean nothing more than "the grave" in some places. But in other places it clearly refers to the realm of departed spirits.

In the progress and unfolding of divine revelation, the New Testament is much more specific. The New Testament reveals that the underworld is a literal place divided into at least four parts. We know this because there are four different words in the Greek New Testament to describe this realm. And I believe each of these words describes a unique division, part, or section of the netherworld.

Let's look together at each of these words to discover their significance.

THE ABYSS OR BOTTOMLESS PIT

One part or section of the underworld is called the abyss, bottomless pit, or the shaft of the abyss. The term *abussos* occurs nine times in the Greek New Testament (Luke 8:31; Romans 10:17; Revelation 9:1, 2, 11; 11:7; 17:8; 20:1, 3).

Evidently, from its description in the Bible, the abyss is a place where a specific group of demons is presently confined, who will be released for a period of five months during the Tribulation to afflict the lost (Revelation 9:1–5). It is also the place where Satan will be bound temporarily for a thousand years during the millennial kingdom (Revelation 20:1–3).

When Jesus was on earth, there was an occasion when he was confronted by a man possessed or "demonized" by a legion of demons. The demons inside the man immediately recognized the presence of the Son of God. "Seeing Jesus, he cried out and fell before Him, and said in a loud voice, 'What business do we have with each other, Jesus, Son of the Most High God? I beg You, do not torment me'" (Luke 8:28).

When it became clear to the demons that Jesus was going to exorcise them from the man, they begged him not to command them to depart into the *abyss,* but rather to allow them to enter into a herd of swine (vv. 31–32). This passage further confirms that the abyss is a temporary place of confinement for some demons who go too far in their rebellion against God. The fear of being cast into the abyss acts as a kind of deterrent or restraint on the scope and extent of their wickedness.

TARTARUS

The word *Tartarus* occurs only one time in the Greek New Testament, in 2 Peter 2:4. "For if God did not spare angels when they sinned, but cast them into hell and committed them to pits of darkness, reserved for judgment." In our English translation, the words "cast them into hell" translate the one Greek word *tartarosas*. In other words, the Bible says that God "tartarized" these angels who sinned, or sent them to tartarus.

In Greek mythology, tartarus was the lowest level of the underworld—the bottom chamber, or basement. It was the place reserved for the most heinous offenders.

In the context of 2 Peter 2:4–8, it seems that Tartarus is a permanent place of confinement for a particular group of angels who sinned in the days of Noah. Notice in the context that Peter mentions these sinning angels (v. 4), then the flood of Noah's day recorded in Genesis 6–8 (v. 5), and then the judgment of Sodom and Gomorrah in the days of Lot recorded in Genesis 18–19 (vv. 6–8). There is a chronological progression through some of the key events in the book of Genesis. Taking this into account, the sins of these angels must have occurred before the flood in the book of Genesis. The only account that could possibly fit this terrible sin is Genesis 6:1–4.

While the subject will probably always remain an item of

debate, there are five key reasons why I believe the "sons of God" in Genesis 6:1–4 are fallen angels who came down to pollute and corrupt the human race to prevent the coming of a fully human Messiah.

First, the phrase "sons of God" *(bene elohim)* is used consistently to refer to angels (Job 1:6; 2:1; 38:7)

Second, the Septuagint, which is the Greek translation of the Old Testament, translated the phrase *bene elohim* in Genesis 6 as "angels of God."

Third, this view is the oldest and most widely held view. The colorful first century Jewish historian Flavius Josephus, as well as almost all other ancient Jewish writers and interpreters, held this position. Also, the earliest Christian writers held to the fallen angel view, including Justin Martyr, Clement of Alexandria, Origen, Irenaeus, Cyprian, Tertullian, Ambrose, Methodius, and others. This view was also promulgated in many pseudopigraphal works such as 1 Enoch, Jubilees, and the Apocalypse of Baruch.

Fourth, this view is substantiated by Jude 1:6–7 which parallels the passage in 2 Peter 2:4. Jude 1:6–7 says:

> And angels who did not keep their own domain, but abandoned their proper abode, He has kept in eternal bonds under darkness for the judgment of the great day, just as Sodom and Gomorrah and the cities around them, since they in the same way as these indulged in gross immorality and went after strange flesh, are exhibited as an example in undergoing the punishment of eternal fire.

These angels committed gross immorality and went after strange flesh just like the people of Sodom and Gomorrah. Some sexual sin by these angels is clearly in view.

The one main objection that is usually leveled against this

view is that angels are sexless beings, or that it's impossible to mix angels and humans. Support for this is drawn from Matthew 22:30 which says that in heaven people will be like the angels of God in heaven in that they won't marry. This passage, however, does not say that people in heaven will lose their personal identity, including male and female gender. And the statement in Matthew 22:30 refers only to unfallen angels in heaven. It doesn't say that fallen angels or demons are incapable of this. Remember also that in the cases in Scripture when angels materialize, they often do carry out the functions of normal human bodies. They eat, drink, walk, and talk.

For these reasons, then, I believe that tartarus is a special place in the underworld where these specific fallen angels or demons are being held until the final day of judgment at the great white throne (Revelation 20:11–15). While the fallen angels in the abyss undergo *temporary* confinement, since they will be released for a while during the tribulation period, tartarus is a place of *permanent* confinement until the great white throne. The angels who committed the monstrous sin in Genesis 6:1–4 are being held permanently until they are finally cast in the lake of fire. They are "committed to pits of darkness, reserved for judgment" (2 Peter 2:4).

HADES

The Greek word *hades* occurs ten times in the New Testament (Matthew 11:23; 16:18; Luke 10:15; 16:23; Acts 2:7, 31; 1 Corinthians 15:55; Revelation 1:18; 6:8; 20:13–14). In a couple of places hades may mean nothing more than just the grave (Acts 2:7, 31). In these cases it's similar in use to the Old Testament word *Sheol.* The majority of the uses of hades in the New Testament, however, reveal that it is the place where the souls of lost people are presently confined while they await the final day of judgment.

Hades is like the county jail where inmates await their trial date, final sentence, and transfer to the penitentiary or prison where they will serve their time.

GEHENNA

The most commonly used term for the underworld or netherworld in the New Testament is the word *gehenna*. It's found twelve times in the Greek New Testament (Matthew 5:22, 29–30; 10:28; 18:9; 23:15, 33; Mark 9:43, 45, 47; Luke 12:5; James 3:6). When we think of the idea of "hell" as it's commonly used, as the final place of torment for fallen angels and unbelieving humans, gehenna is the place we have in mind. In its fullest sense, gehenna is hell.

If hades is the county jail, then gehenna is the maximum-security penitentiary. Gehenna is the final place of torment for Satan, demons, and all the lost people of all the ages (Revelation 20:10, 14–15).

The word *gehenna* comes from the Valley of Hinnom that was just west of the city of Jerusalem. This valley was used in the days of wicked King Ahaz as a place to offer child sacrifices to the god Molech (2 Kings 16:2–3). Later, during the reign of the good king Josiah, he condemned the valley by making it the city dump. It was filled with refuse, worms, maggots, and neverending smoldering fires. This is the imagery behind Jesus' use of this word. Gehenna is also referred to as "the lake of fire and brimstone" (Revelation 20:10), "the lake of fire" (v. 14), and "the second death" (vv. 6, 14). It is called the second death because it is a place of final, eternal separation from God.

It's the place where all the inhabitants of the abyss, tartarus, and hades will ultimately be cast.

Conclusion

To put this all together, the underworld that we often refer to simply as "hell" really has four parts. To avoid confusion, we could use these four designations when referring to the parts of hell or the netherworld:

- abyss hell
- tartarus hell
- hades hell
- gehenna hell

Abyss Hell	Tartarus Hell	Hades Hell	Gehenna Hell (Lake of Fire)
Place of *temporary* confinement of some demons	Place of *permanent* confinement of some demons until the final judgment	Place of confinement for lost people from the time of death until the final judgment	Place of *eternal* judgment for Satan, all demons, and all lost people

Chapter 17

HOW CAN A LOVING GOD SEND PEOPLE TO HELL?

A ny thinking person must admit that the biblical doctrine of hell is difficult. It runs across the grain of man's way of thinking. Let's face it, man wants to believe that a loving God will welcome all of His creatures into heaven. But as we have seen, the Word of God clearly teaches a literal place called hell. The question always comes up: Can a loving God really send people to such a horrible place?

The answer to this question requires us to do some careful thinking about the nature of God. First, the Bible teaches us that God is infinitely holy and just. When people ask, "If God is so loving, how can He send anyone to hell?" we could just as easily ask, "If God is so just, how can He let anyone into heaven?"

You see, the Bible teaches that when God placed Adam and Eve in the garden He gave them only one restriction. They could eat freely from all the trees of the garden, but they could not eat from the fruit of the tree of the knowledge of good and evil, for in the day they ate of it they would surely die (Genesis 2:16–17). Of course, you know the story. Adam and Eve disobeyed God and brought the entire race down in their sin. And a holy, righteous God had to execute the sentence He had decreed upon sin. God's holiness demanded that He judge sin and that sinners be punished for their transgression. "The wages of sin is death" (Romans 6:23).

Second, while it is true that God is infinitely just, it is also true that God is infinitely loving, merciful, good, gracious, and kind. It is as though God found Himself in a dilemma or conflict within His very nature. That conflict, which poses the greatest mystery in the world, is stated clearly in Romans 3:26. How can God on the one hand be just and punish human sin and yet on the other hand justify sinners?

We find the answer to this dilemma of the ages in the cross of Jesus Christ. God poured out the full measure of His wrath against all human sin on His own Son, as He hung on that cross. Jesus died as a substitute in our place, paying the penalty we deserve, tasting death for every person (Hebrews 2:9). Jesus drank the full cup of God's wrath for you and me. He suffered hell or eternal separation from God for us. He paid our sin debt in full (John 19:30). He forever satisfied the wrath, justice, and holiness of God concerning the sin question, allowing God to respond in love and grace to those who accept His Son.

At the cross, God's infinite justice and infinite love met. Both are fully satisfied. For this reason, God can receive the one who simply does nothing more than believe in Christ as his or her substitute (John 1:12). But if we refuse God's gracious offer of salvation through His Son, we have to pay the price for our own sin.

That's the choice. Accept God's love and Christ's payment for your sin and go to heaven. Or, reject it and face God's justice by paying the price yourself in hell. Receive God's love or face God's wrath. The choice is simple, yet eternal. Grace or justice. Which will it be?

I like the way William Lane Craig states it:

> That's why Jesus is the key, and life's supreme question becomes, "What will you do with Christ?" In order to receive forgiveness, we need to place our trust in Christ as our Savior and the Lord of our lives. But if we reject Christ, then we reject God's mercy and fall back on His justice. And you know where you stand there. If we reject Jesus' offer of forgiveness, then there simply is *no one else* to pay the penalty for your sin—except yourself. Thus, in a sense, God doesn't send anybody to hell. His desire is that everyone be saved, and He pleads with people to come to Him. But if we reject Christ's sacrifice for our sin, then God has no choice but to give us what we deserve. God will not send us to hell—but we will send ourselves.[35]

This is the real truth we must face. Sinners send themselves to hell. Of course, God is the Great Judge who consigns people to their self-chosen fate. But ultimately it is man's own doing.

The doctrine of hell is a difficult doctrine. It's one we like to ignore. But may the Lord help us to remember the bad news as an incentive to share the Good News.

As William Lane Craig concludes, "No Christian likes the doctrine of hell. I truly wish with all my heart that universal salvation were true. But to pretend that people are not sinful and in need of salvation would be as cruel and deceptive as pretending that somebody was healthy even though you knew that he had a fatal disease for which you knew the cure."[36]

May God help us to accept that cure for ourselves and faithfully share it with others.

Chapter 18

IS HELL IN THE CENTER OF THE EARTH?

Back in the days of the Soviet Union, I remember reading a report in a newspaper about a drilling expedition in Siberia. The account told of a group of scientists who drilled a hole in the crust of the earth and then claimed to hear the screaming voices of hell. This incident became widely publicized in Christian circles as a proof that hell actually exists.

It became known as the "Hole to Hell."

The details of the story were reportedly from the translation of an article in a Finnish newspaper named *Ammennusatia*. Here is one of the many accounts of the story.

A geological group who drilled a hole about 14.4 kilometers deep in the crust of the earth are saying that they heard human screams. Screams have been heard from the condemned souls from earth's deepest hole. Terrified scientists are afraid they have let loose the evil powers of hell up to the earth's surface.

"The information we are gathering is so surprising, that we are sincerely afraid of what we might find down there," stated Dr Azzacov, the manager of the project in remote Siberia.

The second surprise was the high temperature they discovered in the earth's center. "The calculations indicate the given temperature was about 1,100 degrees Celsius, or over 2,000 degrees Fahrenheit," Azzacov pointed out. "This is far more than we expected. It seems almost like an inferno of fire is brutally going on in the center of the earth.

"The last discovery was nevertheless the most shocking to our ears, so much so that the scientists are afraid to continue the project. We tried to listen to the earth's movements at certain intervals with supersensitive microphones, which were let down through the hole. What we heard turned those logically thinking scientists into a trembling ruins. It was a sometimes weak but high-pitched sound which we thought to be coming from our own equipment," explained Dr Azzacov.

Anyone who had read this far in the Finnish newsman's account would not be able to set the newspaper aside—even if he or she wanted to. And indeed, the story became more eerie and frightening as it went along.

"But after some adjustments we comprehended that indeed the sound came from the earth's interior. We could hardly believe our own ears. We heard a human voice, screaming in pain. Even though one voice was discernible, we could hear thousands, perhaps millions, in the background, of suffering souls screaming. After this ghastly discovery, about half of the scientists quit because of fear. Hopefully, that which is down there will stay there," Dr. Azzacov added.

What really unnerved the Soviets, apart from the voice recordings, was the appearance that same night of a fountainhead of luminous gas shooting up from the drill site, and out of the midst of this incandescent cloud pillar a brilliant being with bat wings revealed itself with the words (in Russian): "I have conquered," emblazoned against the dark Siberian sky.

"The incident was absolutely unreal; the Soviets cried out in terror," says Mr. Nummedal. Later that night, he saw ambulance crews circulating in the community. A driver he knew told him that they had been told to sedate everybody with a medication known to erase short-term memory. The Soviets use this drug in the treatment of shock victims.[37]

Of course, this whole incident was later debunked as just another of many popular urban legends that often take off like wildfire. It was a complete fabrication. The story continued to move from one place to another like falling dominoes because small publications continued to quote each other's unsubstantiated stories. When the trail of the story was traced back, the source for the original story was undetermined, but clearly false.

Another story from 1992 claimed that thirteen oil workers were killed in Alaska when the devil came roaring up out of the ground.

These kinds of stories should serve as an excellent reminder for us all. Our proof for hell doesn't come from drilling operations or people who claim to have been to hell and lived to tell about it.

We get our revelation concerning the afterlife from God's Word.

Hell is usually known as the underworld or netherworld, which conveys the idea that it's under the surface of the earth. The Bible never tells us the specific location of hell, but a few passages in Scripture suggest that hell is in the center of the earth. For instance, Numbers 16:32–33 records this terrifying scene of God's judgment on a rebellious family in Israel:

> And the earth opened its mouth and swallowed them up, and their households, and all the men who belonged to Korah with their possessions. So they and all that belonged to them went down alive to Sheol; and the earth closed over them, and they perished from the midst of the assembly.

A second passage often used in this light is Philippians 2:10, which says, "That at the name of Jesus every knee will bow, of those who are in heaven and on earth and under the earth." In this passage, Paul was making the point that all intelligent creation will one day bow the knee in submission to Jesus Christ. Those in heaven would be believers and unfallen angels, those on earth would be saved and unsaved people during Christ's reign, and those under the earth would be lost people and fallen angels, or demons. In other words, all angels, humans, and demons will bow to Christ and confess His lordship someday.

The purpose of this passage, of course, was not to give the specific location of hell, but rather to say that all intelligent creation will bow to Christ. The phrase "under the earth"—one word in Greek—is used in contrast to "in heaven." Of course, this may have been an accommodation to the thinking of the Philippians—a simple way to communicate to a Greek audience. Their mythology would have taught them that the abode of lost people was subterranean, or under the earth. The word Paul used for "under the earth" *(katachthonios)* was the very same word used in Greek mythology to denote the underworld.[38]

Proponents of the idea that hell is in the center of the earth also quote from another of Paul's letters. In Ephesians 4:9–10, the apostle states that before Jesus ascended to heaven, He first descended into the "lower parts of the earth." In this passage, however, the phrase "lower parts of the earth" is most likely a simple reference to the grave. Paul is saying that before Jesus could ascend to heaven and give gifts to the body of Christ, He first had to die and be buried in the grave ("the lower parts of the earth"). His ascension could not occur before His death.[39]

Yet another serious problem with locating gehenna or the lake of fire in the center of the earth is the clear Bible teaching that Christ will destroy this present heaven and earth following His thousand-year reign in Jerusalem. At that time, He will judge all the lost at the great white throne (Revelation 20:1–15). Since gehenna is eternal and cannot be destroyed, it can't be in the earth, which *will* be destroyed.

In response to this, someone might point out that hades, the abyss, and tartarus will all be emptied of their occupants at the Great White Throne Judgment when the earth is destroyed. It could still be possible, then, that these parts of the netherworld could be located in some sense in the center of the earth. Since the inhabitants of these places are bodiless spirits, however, it seems best not to try to assign some spatial location to any parts of the underworld.

The Bible is clear that a real place called hell—hades, the abyss, tartarus, and the lake of fire—does exist. As to the specific location, however, all we can say for sure is that it is somewhere in God's boundless universe. As part of the unseen world, hell probably exists in some dimension outside the three dimensions of our physical world.

Chapter 19

WILL PEOPLE IN HELL EVER HAVE A SECOND CHANCE?

Some people hold out the idea that those who die without faith in Jesus Christ will somehow, some way, be given another chance to enter into salvation. One final shot after death to get into heaven. A way of escape from the horrors of hell.

Two main New Testament passages are often used to support this notion, both in the book of 1 Peter. The first is 1 Peter 3:18–20.

> For Christ also died for sins once for all, the just for the unjust, in order that He might bring us to God, having been put to death in the flesh, but made alive in the spirit; in which also He went and made proclamation to the spirits now in prison, who once were disobedient, when the patience of God kept waiting in the days of

Noah, during the construction of the ark, in which a few, that is, eight persons, were brought safely through the water.

While this difficult text could be interpreted in several different ways, it cannot mean that Jesus went and preached the gospel to people in hell to give them a second chance at salvation. We know this because it would contradict Jesus' own teaching on this topic in Luke 16:26, where He says that those in hell can never cross the great yawning chasm between heaven and hell. I believe 1 Peter 3:18–20 teaches that between His death and resurrection Jesus went to tartarus and proclaimed His victory over sin to the demons confined there.[40] His triumph on the cross sealed their eternal doom (see Colossians 2:15). It was bad news to them but a message of comfort and encouragement to God's people.

The second passage often used to support the notion of a second chance for salvation after death is 1 Peter 4:6. "For the gospel has for this purpose been preached even to those who are dead, that though they are judged in the flesh as men, they may live in the spirit according to the will of God." This passage, however, simply means that deceased believers who had the gospel preached to them received it while they were still alive.[41]

As much as people might hold out hope for an escape route from hell, the Bible is clear that no such escape route exists. As M. R. DeHaan put it, "Once we have passed through the door of death, we can't pick up our suitcase and move out because we don't like the accommodations."[42]

Nothing can change one's fate after death. There is no purgatory, no second chance, no parole for good behavior, and no graduation. As the old saying goes, "As death finds us, eternity keeps us. Hell is truth seen too late."

The lost can never come to heaven, and the saved can never end up in hell. Remember Abraham's words from heaven to the rich man in hades: "And besides all this, between us and you there is a great chasm fixed, so that those who wish to come over from here to you will not be able, and that none may cross over from there to us" (Luke 16:26). Jesus Himself made it clear that no one from hades will ever have an opportunity to move from that place of torment to heaven or paradise. Hell is a place of destiny!

About a mile off the coast of San Francisco in the bay sits the solitary island of Alcatraz, a former federal prison for the worst of criminals. I have visited that island prison three times. Alcatraz was notorious for being a place from which there was no hope of escape. The tightest security one could imagine smothered the island. And even if you could somehow get outside the walls, you still faced the surrounding frigid waters with strong currents and sharks.

My sons and I love the 1979 movie *Escape from Alcatraz,* starring Clint Eastwood. It tells the story of the escape from the "rock" by Frank Morris and John and Clarence Anglin on June 12, 1962. Most experts believe the cold, strong current probably carried the three men out to the Pacific Ocean, where they drowned. They are presumed to be dead. But interestingly, their bodies were never recovered. As difficult as it was, at least three men escaped from Alcatraz.

But hell is the true inescapable prison. It's a prison house surrounded not by freezing water but by a lake of fire. No one can free himself of its clutches.

I heard a story about W. C. Fields when he was on his deathbed. He was feverishly looking through a Bible. One of the people there with him said, "I didn't know you were a religious man."

"I'm not," Fields replied.

The man said, "Then what are you doing?"

"Looking for loopholes!" said Fields.

My friend, there are no loopholes. Not today. Not ever. God has spoken. Jesus is the way, the truth, and the life; no one comes to the Father but by Him (John 14:6). Receive Him today. "Now is 'the acceptable time,' behold, now is 'the day of salvation'" (2 Corinthians 6:2).

There will be no second chance after you leave this earth.

Now's your opportunity.

Chapter 20

WILL HELL REALLY LAST FOREVER?

The doctrine of hell is undoubtedly the most disturbing subject in the Bible, and the most disturbing truth about hell is its duration. The idea of people being punished for their sins and misdeeds doesn't bother most people. But the notion that hell will last *forever* is totally repugnant. For this reason, many have tried to soften this truth by adopting a "kinder, gentler" view of hell. They do this in spite of the fact that the Bible refers to eternal judgment as one of the elementary teachings of the Bible (Hebrews 6:1–2). Eternal judgment of the lost in hell is part of the spiritual ABCs every believer should understand and believe.

Two erroneous views of the fate of the lost have become popular in recent years. The first of these views is *annihilationism,* which teaches that all souls are immortal, but that the wicked lose their immortality at the final judgment and are extinguished by God. For annihilationists, the punishment for the lost is eternal extinction.

The second incorrect view is *conditional immortality,* which teaches that human souls are not inherently immortal and that at the judgment the wicked pass into oblivion while the righteous are given immortality.

These two ideas are so similar to each other that they are usually not distinguished from one another. The views are normally merged together for the sake of simplicity and termed annihilationism.

Advocates of annihilationism put forward two main arguments. First, they contend that the lost are "destroyed" or cease to exist either at death or some later time determined by God. Matthew 10:28 is one of the verses they appeal to. "Do not fear those who kill the body but are unable to kill the soul; but rather fear Him who is able to destroy both soul and body in hell."

The Greek word *appolumi /apoleia,* which is translated "destroyed" most often in the New Testament, means to ruin, waste, destroy, or lose. In Mark 14:4 it means "to waste." In Luke 15 it's used eight times and means "lost." The coin, sheep, and son are lost, but obviously still exist.

The second argument annihilationists use is that the *punishment* of the lost is eternal, but not the *punishing.* In other words, the fires of hell will burn forever, but the lost will not be there to endure them.

While annihilationism is certainly more appealing to the human mind than the traditional view of eternal damnation in hell, the Bible clearly teaches that punishment in hell will last forever.

The Greek word *aionios,* which is translated "eternal" or "everlasting," is used seventy-one times in the New Testament. Fifty-one times it is used of the happiness of the saved in heaven. It is used of both the quality and quantity of life that believers will experience with God. The word is used another two times of the duration of God in His glory (Romans 16:26; 1 Timothy 6:16).

One time it's used of the duration of the glorified bodies of believers in heaven (2 Corinthians 5:1). Several other times it is used in such a way that no one would question that it means forever. Seven times it is used of the fate of the wicked, and there should be no doubt to an objective mind that in these passages the word means eternal, forever, or without end (Matthew 18:8; 25:41, 46; Mark 3:29; 2 Thessalonians 1:9; Hebrews 6:2; Jude 1:7).

One of the clearest references in the New Testament to the eternality of punishment in hell is Revelation 14:10–11:

"He also will drink of the wine of the wrath of God, which is mixed in full strength in the cup of His anger; and he will be tormented with fire and brimstone in the presence of the holy angels and in the presence of the Lamb. And the smoke of their torment goes up forever and ever; they have no rest day and night, those who worship the beast and his image, and whoever receives the mark of his name."

In Matthew 25:46, in the same verse, both heaven and hell are described as "eternal": "These will go away into eternal punishment, but the righteous into eternal life." To limit the meaning of eternal for the damned, one must also be willing to limit it for the saved as well.

Mark 9:47–48 indicates that punishment and punishing in hell is eternal. "Cast into hell, where their worm does not die, and the fire is not quenched." Why would the fire in hell be eternal if no one will be there forever?

Revelation 20:10 reinforces the teaching of eternal punishment in hell. "And the devil who deceived them was thrown into the lake of fire and brimstone, where the beast and false prophet are also; and they will be tormented day and night forever and ever." This passage makes it clear that the torment itself is eternal. The great Lutheran commentator R. C. H. Lenski says:

> The strongest expression for our "forever" is *eis tous aionan ton aionon,* "for the eons of eons"; each of vast duration, are multiplied by many more, which we imitate by "forever and ever." Human language is able to use only temporal terms to express what is altogether beyond time and timeless. The Greek takes its greatest term for time, the eon, pluralizes this, and then multiplies it by its own plural, even using articles which make the eons the definite ones.[43]

The same phrase of duration is used numerous times of the duration of God's existence (Revelation 1:18; 4:9–10; 10:6; 15:7).

The eternality of hell is sobering indeed. I copied these words from a sermon by Charles Spurgeon many years ago. They powerfully express the terror and heart-wrenching despair of the eternality of hell.

> In hell there is no hope. They have not even the hope of dying; the hope of being annihilated. They are forever, forever, forever lost. On every chain in hell is written "forever." Up above their heads they read "forever." Their eyes are galled and their hearts are pained with the thought that it is "forever." Oh, if I could tell you tonight that hell would one day be burned out, and that those who were lost might be saved, there would be a jubilee in hell at the very thought of it. But it cannot be. It is "forever." They are "cast into outer darkness."[44]

Knowing the terrible, everlasting judgment that awaits the lost should cause us to plead with them to be reconciled to God (2 Corinthians 5:20–21).

The real Achilles' heel of the annihilation view is the truth of degrees of punishment in hell. Obviously, there would be no need for degrees of annihilation. Either you are annihilated or you aren't. Let's turn now to the issue of degrees or levels of punishment in hell.

Chapter 21

WILL EVERYONE BE PUNISHED THE SAME IN HELL?

Since God is a God of justice and righteousness, the punishment of sinners must fit the crime. The Bible teaches that there will be degrees of punishment in hell for unbelievers based on the amount and nature of the sin committed and the light that was refused. Jesus Himself taught that there will be degrees of punishment in hell. Here is just some of what Jesus had to say on this topic.

> "Truly I say to you, it will be more tolerable for the land of Sodom and Gomorrah in the day of judgment than for that city." (Matthew 10:15).

Then He began to denounce the cities in which most of His miracles were done, because they did not repent. "Woe to you, Chorazin! Woe to you, Bethsaida! For if the miracles had occurred in Tyre and Sidon which occurred in you, they would have repented long ago in sackcloth and ashes. Nevertheless I say to you, it will be more tolerable for Tyre and Sidon in the day of judgment than for you. And you, Capernaum, will not be exalted to heaven, will you? You will descend to Hades; for if the miracles had occurred in Sodom which occurred in you, it would have remained to this day. Nevertheless I say to you that it will be more tolerable for the land of Sodom in the day of judgment, than for you." (Matthew 11:20–24).

"The master of that slave will come on a day when he does not expect him and at an hour he does not know, and will cut him in pieces, and assign him a place with the unbelievers. And that slave who knew his master's will and did not get ready or act in accord with his will, will receive many lashes, but the one who did not know it, and committed deeds worthy of a flogging, will receive but few. From everyone who has been given much, much will be required; and to whom they entrusted much, of him they will ask all the more." (Luke 12:46–48)

The degrees of punishment given by the Lord will be declared at a solemn event known as the Great White Throne Judgment. The sobering scene is set forth in Revelation 20:11–15:

Then I saw a great white throne and Him who sat upon it, from whose presence earth and heaven fled away, and no place was found for them. And I saw the dead, the great and the small, standing before the throne, and books were opened; and another book was opened, which is the book of life; and the dead were judged from the things which were written in the books according to their deeds. And the sea gave up the dead which were in it, and death and Hades gave up the dead which were in them; and they were judged, every one of them according to their deeds. Then death and Hades were thrown into the lake of fire. This is the second death, the lake of fire. And if anyone's name was not found written in the book of life, he was thrown into the lake of fire.

The Great White Throne Judgment is for unbelievers only. All the lost of all the ages will be summoned by God to appear before His almighty bar of justice. And all who appear at the Great White Throne Judgment will be declared guilty, and all will get "life," or actually an eternal "death" sentence, but the severity of the sentences will vary.

At the Great White Throne Judgment the Lord will open "the book" and "the books." From the context it seems clear that the "book" (singular) is the Lamb's Book of Life that contains the names of all God's elect down through the ages. The names of those who stand before the great white throne will not be found in that book. But the "books" (plural) contain the names and all the deeds of the lost (Revelation 20:11–12). From these books, the Lord will tailor the exact punishment to meet the crime.

One thing this teaches us is that hell is earned. "The wages of sin is death" (Romans 6:23). We all deserve to go there.

But heaven is free.

With this in mind, let's turn now from the underworld to the other world.

From the bad news to the best news.

From hell to heaven.

From torture to triumph.

PART FOUR

Our
Heavenly
Home

Chapter 22

IS HEAVEN
A REAL PLACE?

If you've been reading this book straight through, I'm sure you're ready for a change of subject about now. I know I am. I'm so grateful that hell doesn't have the last word…that there's a place called heaven that Jesus is preparing for His people. But not everyone agrees.

Sadly, some today seem to have adopted the John Lennon view of the afterlife made popular in his song: "Imagine there's no heaven; it's easy if you try. No hell below us—above us only sky."

But the vast majority of Americans believe in a real place called heaven. In a *Time* magazine cover article titled "Does Heaven Exist?" people were asked various questions about heaven. Here are a few of the questions and responses:

Do you believe in the existence of heaven, where people live forever with God after they die?

Yes	81 percent
No	13 percent

Where do you believe you will go when you die?

Heaven	68 percent
Hell	3 percent

The fact of a literal place called heaven permeates the pages of God's Word. The word *heaven* occurs about 550 times in the Bible. It is a general word that is used to describe three different "heavens" that exist. The first heaven is the atmospheric heaven, the abode of the birds. The second heaven is the stellar or celestial heaven, the home of the sun, moon, planets, and stars. The third heaven is the divine heaven, the abode of God. Contrary to popular belief, there is no *seventh* heaven.

When we talk about heaven, we are usually referring to the divine heaven, or third heaven—the dwelling place of God. The Bible tells us that this third heaven is just as real as the first and second heavens we can see.

There are six reasons why I believe heaven is a literal place that exists right now.

1. Jesus called heaven "My Father's house" and said He was going there to prepare a "place" for His people (John 14:1–3). Heaven, according to Jesus, is a real place.

2. Heaven is described as a literal place, a city, with walls, gates, foundations, and a street in majestic, glorious, enthralling detail in Revelation 21:9–22:5. The Bible begins man's existence in a garden that was a literal place (the Garden of Eden) and ends in a city, the New Jerusalem, that is also a real place.

3. Jesus taught that heaven is the present abode or dwelling place of God (Matthew 10:32–33).

4. The apostle Paul visited the "third heaven" where God dwells (2 Corinthians 12:2).

5. The true citizenship of every Christian is in heaven (Philippians 3:20–21). You can't have legitimate citizenship in a place that doesn't exist.

6. Heaven is called our heavenly homeland and a city (Hebrews 11:16).

Heaven is a real place. It's a prepared place for a prepared people.

Chapter 23

WHAT ARE SOME OF THE OTHER NAMES FOR HEAVEN?

Here's a brief list of some of the more common biblical terms or names for the place we call heaven.

TEN BIBLICAL NAMES FOR HEAVEN

1. My Father's House (John 14:2).
2. The City of the Living God (Hebrews 12:22).
3. Mount Zion (Hebrews 12:22).
4. The Heavenly Jerusalem (Hebrews 12:22; Revelation 21:2).
5. Paradise (Luke 23:43; 2 Corinthians 12:4; Revelation 2:7).
6. The Third Heaven (2 Corinthians 12:2).
7. A Better Country (Hebrews 11:16).
8. A Heavenly Homeland (Hebrews 11:16).
9. A Heavenly City (Hebrews 11:16).
10. The Holy City (Revelation 21:2).

Chapter 24

WHY SHOULD WE SPEND TIME THINKING ABOUT HEAVEN?

Many people today spend little or no time thinking about the hereafter. The prevailing attitude today seems to be "heaven can wait." You even find this attitude overtaking the church as well. In churches there is little talk about heaven. No singing about heaven. No excitement about heaven. I even hear Christians sometimes say that you can be so heavenly minded you're of no earthly good.

Marty Marty, the respected University of Chicago religious historian, says, "I can recall from my [Lutheran] childhood many sermons on what used to be called the geography of heaven and the temperature of hell. Now the only time you hear of heaven is when somebody has died."[45]

David Wells, a theology professor at Gordon-Conwell Theological Seminary, notes, "We would expect to hear of it in the Evangelical churches, but I don't hear it at all. I don't think heaven is even a blip on the Christian screen, from one end of the denominational spectrum to the other."[46]

But this is not the picture the Bible paints about our attitude toward heaven. God's Word says heaven is our eternal home. We will live there forever, and we should be deeply interested in what it is like. God's Word devotes the bulk of its last two chapters to the subject of heaven (Revelation 21:1–22:5).

Most people go on some kind of vacation every year. Probably at least once your family has planned a great vacation to a place you didn't know much about. What did you do to prepare for the trip? You did an Internet search, looked at maps, read about the key sites in the area, found out about the best restaurants and hotels, and did your best to learn some of the local customs.

Think about it. You did all that planning and learning for just a few weeks of vacation. But we will be in heaven *forever*. Don't you want to know what your heavenly home will be like?

Almost everyone at one time or another has moved to a new area or new city. What do you do when you finally decide you are moving? You visit the new area. You check out the neighborhoods, the schools, the climate, the churches, the restaurants, the athletic fields, the shopping areas, the entertainment, and so on. You discover everything you can about the new place. Why? Because you are moving there. It's going to be your new home.

Again, heaven will be our eternal home. It's only natural that we should want to know all we can about the place where we will spend eternity.

For that matter, God's Word implores us, "Set your mind on the things above, not on the things that are on earth" (Colossians 3:2). Thinking about heaven has at least five practical effects on our lives here on earth.

1. Focusing on heaven restores our hope in times of suffering (Romans 8:18).
2. Focusing on heaven reassures us that God is on the throne (Revelation 4:1–3).
3. Focusing on heaven reminds us that this world is not our home (Philippians 3:20).
4. Focusing on heaven refocuses our attention on the nature of true treasure (Matthew 6:19–21).
5. Focusing on heaven reignites our fervor to serve the Lord (Isaiah 6:1–8).

Being heavenly minded is really the only thing that will make us of any earthly good.

C. S. Lewis had it right:

If you read history you will find that the Christians who did the most for the present world were just those who thought most of the next. The Apostles themselves, who set on foot the conversion of the Roman Empire, the great men who built up the Middle Ages, the English evangelicals who abolished the slave trade, all left their mark on earth, precisely because their minds were occupied with Heaven. It is since Christians have largely ceased to think of the other world that they have become so ineffective in this one.[47]

Or, as I once heard someone wisely say, "Aim at heaven and you will get earth 'thrown in.' Aim at earth and you will get neither."

Chapter 25

WHAT IS HEAVEN LIKE?

People have all kinds of ideas about what heaven is like. In a recent *Newsweek* poll here were a few of the more popular ideas.

- 19 percent believe heaven looks like a garden.
- 13 percent say it looks like a city.
- 17 percent don't know.[48]

A television producer for the British Broadcasting Corporation was preparing a documentary about Christianity in England. In the course of his research, he sent a memo to a clergyman who served as an adviser to the BBC on church affairs.

The memo read, "How might I ascertain the official church view of heaven and hell?" The clergyman replied with a memo consisting of only one word:

"Die."[49]

Fortunately, we do not have to die to discover God's truth about heaven. The Bible is clear that there is a place called heaven where believers will live with God forever. But what else does the Bible tell us about this amazing place? What do we know about what it will be like?

Revelation 21–22 tells us most of what we know about the eternal state or what we call heaven. Even so, these chapters only give us the briefest of glimpses. In that glimpse, however, we encounter five glorious points about what heaven will be like.

1. The splendor of heaven

Heaven will be a glorious, splendid place because of both what *is* there and what *is not* there. Twelve specific things won't be there:

1. no sea (21:1)
2. no sin (21:27)
3. no death (21:4)
4. no mourning (21:4)
5. no crying (21:4)
6. no pain (21:4)
7. no night (21:25)
8. no temple (21:22)
9. no curse or corruption (22:3)
10. no sun (21:23)
11. no moon (21:23)
12. no Satanic opposition (20:10)

The main thing that will be there is the glory of God (Revelation 21:11, 23). Heaven will be a city ablaze with His glory. The dazzling brilliance of the Lord will shine and glimmer off the city like a diamond. I believe this is what will really make heaven, heaven. God in all His glory is there. And the absence of God's glorious presence is what will make hell, hell.

Just being in the presence of the eternal, infinite, majestic, glorious, omnipotent, omniscient, omnipresent One will be bliss the likes of which we can only faintly imagine.

2. The sights of heaven

When we visit a new city we always want to see the key sights. In Revelation 21:9–22:5, John gives us a guided tour of the seven foremost sights in the New Jerusalem.

The Wall	The wall is 216 feet thick and 1,500 miles high (7 million feet). The wall shows that heaven is a place of security.
The Gates	The twelve gates are each made of a single pearl. Each gate is guarded by an angel and inscribed with one of the names of the twelve tribes of Israel. The gates speak of the access of heaven.
The Foundation	The twelve foundation stones each consist of a different precious stone. They are each inscribed with one of the names of the twelve apostles. The foundation gives stability and permanence.
The Street	There is only one street (main street), and it is made of pure gold like transparent glass. The street reveals heaven as a place of movement and travel.
The River	A river runs through it—literally. The river brings eternal refreshment.
The Throne	God is seated on His throne as the monarch of the universe. The throne reveals God's sovereignty and rule.
The Tree	Man was banned from the tree of life in Genesis 3, but access to the tree is restored in the heavenly paradise in Revelation 2:7 and 22:2.

3. The size and shape of heaven

The size of the heavenly city is 1,500 miles on each side—1,500 miles wide, 1,500 miles long, and 1,500 miles high. The moon is 2,160 miles in diameter. So the city is like an enormous floating continent coming down to settle on the new earth.

To put this 1,500 miles in perspective, that's the size of the area from Florida to Maine to Minneapolis to Houston and back to Florida.

The shape of the city is a perfect cube. The city contains 2.25 million square miles or 3,375,000,000 cubic miles of space. It has enough room to accommodate one hundred thousand billion people.

And that's just the city. We will have all of the new earth and new heavens to explore.

The heavenly city, the New Jerusalem, will come down out of heaven to sit on the new earth as the capital city of the new heaven and new earth. So our eternal home will include the heavenly city, the New Jerusalem, as well as the entire new earth God will create and the new heaven, or new universe. So don't ever worry if there will be enough room in heaven.

We will live in the heavenly city. The mansion that Jesus is preparing for us right now will be in the New Jerusalem, so it will always be home for us. But our existence won't be confined to the city. We will be able to go in and out of the New Jerusalem that sits on the earth and move about on the new earth. We will also be able to travel about through trillions and zillions of miles of God's new universe.

Here's a simple diagram that shows the size of the heavenly city and its relationship to the new earth.

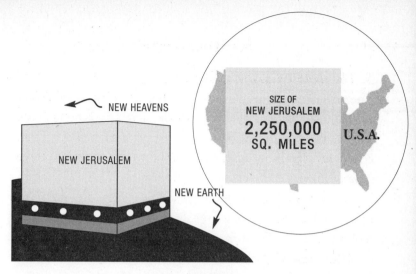

NEW HEAVENS

NEW JERUSALEM

NEW EARTH

SIZE OF
NEW JERUSALEM
2,250,000
SQ. MILES

U.S.A.

Representation taken from Randall Price, **Jerusalem in Prophecy** (Eugene, OR: Harvest House, 1998), 312.

4. The substance of heaven

Heaven won't have any cinder blocks, shag carpet, or budget cutbacks. Only the best materials in the universe will do for the dwelling place of our glorious God. The walls will be of diamond, and the city itself of pure gold. The foundation stones—each one five hundred miles wide—will be diamond, sapphire (blue), chalcedony (greenish blue), emerald (green), sardonyx (layered stone of red and white), sardius (fiery red), chrysolite (golden yellow), beryl (sea green), topaz (greenish yellow), chrysoprase (gold green), jacinth (violet), and amethyst (purple quartz). Each of the twelve massive gates will be made from a single pearl.

The story is told of a Philadelphia law firm that sent flowers to an associate in Baltimore upon hearing of its new offices. Through some mix-up, the ribbon that bedecked the floral piece read "Deepest sympathy."

When the florist was informed of his mistake, he let out a cry of alarm. "Good heavens," he exclaimed, "then the flowers that went to the funeral said, 'Congratulations on your new location!'"[50]

Heaven will be a wonderful new location.

5. *The sanctity of heaven*

There's an old spiritual that says, "Everybody talkin' 'bout heaven ain't goin' there." The sanctity of heaven refers to its holiness, its separation. Heaven will be a sanctified place where no evil will be present. The list of those who will be excluded is found three times in the final two chapters of Revelation (21:8, 27; 22:15). Not everyone will be there.

The only people who will be there are those whose names are found in the Lamb's Book of Life. This book is heaven's register of all the lost sinners who have given up on themselves and trusted Jesus Christ alone to be their Savior from sin.

A few years ago over Valentine's weekend my wife and I went with three other couples on vacation to a resort on the Mayan Riviera near Cancun, Mexico. We left behind the cold, windy, gray weather in Oklahoma for three days of paradise.

The weather was great. The water was beautiful. The grounds of the resort were colorful, lush, and impeccable. The fellowship and relaxation were memorable. But one thing about the trip stood out to me that made the vacation especially enjoyable. The trip was "all-inclusive." What that means is that for one price my wife and I got it all. Everything was included in the one price. Plane tickets, bus ride, room, exercise facilities, spa, taxes, tips, food, drinks. Everything! We never had to think about how much something cost. We didn't have to worry about bringing our wallet or figuring out how much to tip…in pesos. It was all-inclusive.

Now let me assure you Cancun was no heaven on earth. Not even close. But the trip was a brief glimpse of heaven in this sense. It's all-inclusive. In heaven we get it all. Whatever is there is ours for the taking, the enjoying, and absolutely free. You see, the best part of the all-inclusive paradise we call heaven is that the price has already been paid for us by Jesus Christ. He paid the full price with His blood. By receiving Him by faith, we get it all.

Chapter 26

WHAT ABOUT PEOPLE WHO CLAIM TO HAVE VISITED HEAVEN?

In recent years, dozens of books have been written by people who claim to have visited heaven and/or hell and then come to give the rest of us a firsthand preview of what lies beyond this life. Some of these books have hit the bestseller list. Not long ago I heard a man on Christian television relating in great detail his incredible story about his visit to heaven.

There are many problems with these kinds of books and stories that could be mentioned. All of the books on this topic I have looked at contain serious and explicit biblical and theological errors. But let me mention the two main problems with these kinds of books and accounts.

First, those who claim to have visited heaven and then come back to report what they saw are placing themselves in very select company. As far as we know, God reserved this incredible experience for only one Old Testament prophet, Isaiah (Isaiah 6:1–8), and two first-century apostles—Paul and John. Isaiah recorded his experience very briefly and only to tell about his divine call to ministry. And the apostle Paul was not permitted by God to describe his experience. He said he heard "inexpressible words, which a man is not permitted to speak" (2 Corinthians 12:4). In fact, he didn't even mention it until fourteen years after it occurred (v. 2).

The Bible consistently reveals a cautious reserve and reticence to reveal too much about heaven or hell. Stop and think about this. Why would God forbid Paul from telling us about what he saw when he was caught up to paradise and yet let dozens of others in the last twenty years do it? Remember also that because of this unique experience of being allowed to see heaven, God sent Paul a thorn in the flesh to keep him from becoming proud or exalted in his own eyes as a result of receiving this mind-boggling revelation (2 Corinthians 12:7). This thorn in the flesh was evidently some serious physical malady that afflicted Paul. The apostle went from the third heaven to the thorn in the flesh.

What a contrast!

As far as I know none of those who claim to have visited heaven have suffered a debilitating, painful physical problem or "thorn in the flesh" as a result of their experience. If Paul needed this to keep him humble, I'm sure they would need it too.

Second, the Bible strongly warns us not to go beyond the revelation God has given us about heaven or other areas of biblical truth. First Corinthians 4:6 states the important principle that we are "not to exceed what is written" in God's Word.

The book of Revelation contains our best information about heaven. In chapters 4–5 and 21–22, God gave the apostle John this unique unveiling of the future life. But remember, after John received his vision of heaven, God added this sober warning:

> "I testify to everyone who hears the words of the prophecy of this book: if anyone adds to them, God will add to him the plagues which are written in this book; and if anyone takes away from the words of the book of this prophecy, God will take away his part from the tree of life and from the holy city, which are written in this book." (22:18–19)

These are some of the final words of God in the Bible. And last words are lasting words. God is saying that His Word on this subject is enough. It's final. God, in His Word, has given us everything He wants us to know for now about heaven and hell. It's sufficient.

Anyone claiming to know more about heaven than what God revealed to John in Revelation is "adding to" the prophecy of that book, and that is directly forbidden by God.

Stay far away from any book written by someone claiming to have some "special" firsthand information or experience with the afterlife.

Stick with the Bible. It will never lead you astray.

Chapter 27

DOES ST. PETER REALLY SIT AT THE PEARLY GATES OF HEAVEN?

In a *Time* magazine cover article titled "Does Heaven Exist?" people were asked various questions about heaven. In the following question, the pollsters got rather specific. The response tells us a lot about people's general impressions of heaven.

Which of the following do you believe are in heaven?

Angels	93 percent
St. Peter	79 percent
Harps	43 percent
Halos	36 percent

Did you catch that? St. Peter is right behind angels and way ahead of harps and halos. You have certainly heard many jokes about heaven. And how do almost all of them begin? With something about St. Peter sitting at the pearly gates.

One of my favorite jokes in this genre begins with a woman who died and found herself standing outside the pearly gates, being greeted by St. Peter. "Oh!" she exclaimed. "Is this place what I really think it is? It's so beautiful. Did I really make it to heaven?"

To which St. Peter replied, "Yes, my dear, these are the gates to heaven. But you must do one more thing before you can enter." The woman was very excited and asked of St. Peter what she must do to pass through the gates.

"Spell a word," St. Peter replied.

"What word?" she asked. "Any word," answered St. Peter. "It's your choice."

The woman promptly replied, "Then the word I will spell is *love*. L-o-v-e."

St. Peter congratulated her on her good fortune to have made it to heaven and asked her if she would mind taking his place at the gates for a few minutes while he took a break.

"I'd be honored," she said, "but what should I do if someone comes while you are gone?"

St. Peter instructed the woman to simply have any newcomers to the pearly gates spell a word as she had done.

So the woman was left sitting in St. Peter's chair and watching the beautiful angels soaring around her, when lo and behold, a man approached the gates, and she realized it was her husband.

"What happened?" she cried. "Why are you here?"

Her husband stared at her for a moment, then said, "I was so upset when I left your funeral that I was in an accident. And now I am here. Did I really make it to heaven?"

To which the woman replied, "Not yet. You must spell a word first."

"What word?" he asked.

The woman responded, "Czechoslovakia."

We all get a kick out of these kinds of jokes, but we have to ask ourselves—where did this prevalent notion come from? Where did people ever get the idea that the apostle Peter sits at the gates of heaven to determine who is included and who is excluded? And is it biblical?

The role of Peter at the gates of heaven finds its origin in a misunderstanding of Jesus' words to His disciple in Matthew 16:15–19.

> He said to them, "But who do you say that I am?" Simon Peter answered, "You are the Christ, the Son of the living God." And Jesus said to him, "Blessed are you, Simon Barjona, because flesh and blood did not reveal this to you, but My Father who is in heaven. I also say to you that you are Peter, and upon this rock I will build My church; and the gates of Hades will not overpower it. *I will give you the keys of the kingdom of heaven*; and whatever you bind on earth shall have been bound in heaven, and whatever you loose on earth shall have been loosed in heaven."

You can see how someone could read certain words from Matthew 16, which I italicized, and get the idea that Peter has the keys to heaven to determine who gets in and who's excluded. But if you read the context carefully, the keys to the kingdom of heaven have to do with Christ's building of His church on earth—not what Peter supposedly does in heaven. The best way to translate the final phrase of this section is the translation found in the New English Translation: "And whatever you bind on earth will have been bound in heaven, and whatever you release on earth will have been released in heaven." In other words, Peter accomplishes on earth only that which has already been done in heaven.

Keys in that day spoke of authority. The same is true today. If you have the keys to something, then you have authority over it. A car, a home, a boat, a building. What this meant was that Peter was given the privilege, the authority by God, to proclaim the good news of the kingdom—by which entrance into the kingdom would be opened to many who accept it and shut to those who reject it. Peter fulfilled these words of Jesus in Acts 2 on the day of Pentecost, and in Acts 10 at the household of Cornelius. He also fulfilled them in Acts 8 by announcing judgment on Simon Magus.

Those that Peter ushered into the kingdom had already been loosed or released by God in heaven. Peter's actions didn't force heaven to comply with what he did. Rather, he could be authoritative in his actions, knowing that heaven had already acted first (Acts 18:9–10).[51]

With these things in view, Matthew 16 should not be used to support the idea that Peter sits at the pearly gates determining who gets in and who doesn't.

That issue is settled once and for all here on earth by what you do with Jesus Christ.

Chapter 28

WILL PEOPLE IN HEAVEN PLAY HARPS?

For whatever reason, one of the main things people think about when they turn their minds toward heaven is harps. The idea many people have of heaven is of floating along on a big white cloud forever, plucking away at a harp.

As we will discover later, in chapter 36, this is not an accurate view of life in heaven. But it does raise the question: Will we play harps in heaven?

According to the *Time* magazine poll I have quoted several times, 43 percent of Americans believe that harps will be in heaven. Where does this notion come from? Is it biblical?

Actually, it may surprise you to know that there really *will* be harps in heaven. And you may be playing one!

The Greek word for *harp* in the New Testament is *kithara,* from which we get our word *guitar*. The *kithara* was a stringed instrument like a lyre or small modern harp. The harp is employed more than any other instrument in Scripture in the direct worship and praise of God.[52]

The noun and verb form of this word occur six times in the New Testament, and four of them are in Revelation.

The first use is found in Revelation 5:8: "When He had taken the book, the four living creatures and the twenty-four elders fell down before the Lamb, each one holding a harp and golden bowls of incense, which are the prayers of the saints."

Some hold that these twenty-four elders are angelic beings. But I believe that they represent the redeemed, glorified church of Jesus Christ in heaven. If this interpretation is correct, then if you know Jesus Christ as your personal Savior, you and I will play harps in heaven.

In Revelation 15:2, Tribulation saints—those who refused to take the mark of the beast and were martyred for the sake of Christ—are pictured "standing on the sea of glass, holding harps of God."

So the Bible does mention saints in heaven playing harps in direct praise and worship to the Lamb and the One who sits on the throne. This is just another thing to look forward to in heaven. All of God's people will have perfect musical talent.

Strumming a harp certainly isn't all we will do, as some have mistakenly believed, but it will be a glorious part of our praise to the Lord.

Chapter 29

ARE THERE REWARDS IN HEAVEN?

Just as there will be degrees of punishment in hell for the lost, there will also be different degrees of reward in heaven for the Lord's people. Some Christians seem to have a difficult time accepting the idea of God giving rewards to His people for faithful service. To them it turns our service for the Lord into a mercenary activity. Nevertheless (like it or not), the Bible teaches clearly that God *will* reward believers according to our works.

The Bible is clear that God is not only a Judge but also a Rewarder. Consider these numerous passages on the subject of rewards: Psalm 58:11; 62:12; Proverbs 11:18; Isaiah 40:10; 62:11; Matthew 5:12; 6:1–2; 10:41–42; Luke 6:35; 1 Corinthians 3:8, 14; Ephesians 6:8; Hebrews 10:35–36; 11:6, 24–26; 2 John 1:8; Revelation 2:23; 11:18; 22:12.

While many things about heavenly rewards remain a mystery to us, the Bible does tell us some things about God's method of rewarding His people for faithful service. Let's see what the Bible has to say on this intriguing subject.

THE JUDGMENT SEAT OF CHRIST

The rewarding of church-age believers—that is, those who have trusted in Jesus Christ between the day of Pentecost and the Rapture—will occur at what the Bible calls the "judgment seat of Christ" (2 Corinthians 5:10). This judgment will occur in heaven immediately after the Rapture (1 Corinthians 4:5).

The purpose of the judgment seat

Every person reading these words will appear at one of two great future judgments: the judgment *(bema)* seat of Christ or the Great White Throne Judgment. The issue is not *if* we will stand before God, but rather *when* and *where*. And there is no more important issue that you could possibly consider.

The Great White Throne Judgment will occur at the end of the thousand-year reign of Christ on the earth, when all the lost of all the ages will appear before the Lord to be judged for their sins (Revelation 20:11–15). It's for unbelievers.

The judgment seat of Christ is for believers of this age. The purpose is not to determine whether people will enter heaven or hell or to mete out punishment for sin. This ultimate issue was already decided when the person believed in Jesus Christ as Savior. God's Word is clear that His children will never be judged for their sins (John 5:24).

The purpose of the judgment seat of Christ is to review our lives, service, thoughts, words, and motives after we became a Christian and to either give rewards or withhold rewards based on the perfect evaluation of the Lord (Matthew 12:36; 1 Corinthians 4:5; Hebrews 4:13).

The following chart sets forth the contrasts between the judgment seat of Christ and the Great White Throne Judgment.

	The Judgment Seat of Christ	The Great White Throne Judgment
Who?	Church age believers	Unbelievers of every age
Where?	In heaven	In space—heaven and earth flee
When?	After the Rapture	After the thousand-year reign of Christ
What?	Reward	Judgment

The preparation for the judgment seat

It doesn't take very long in school to realize that the most important day is test day. When a major test looms, everything changes. The mood and atmosphere undergo instant transformation. Kids who have been talking and goofing around one minute suddenly get serious when the teacher begins to give a preview of questions on the upcoming exam. Everyone begins to listen attentively. Knowing the questions ahead of time takes a huge weight off of your shoulders.

The Bible tells us that the great test day for our lives as God's children is coming. But like a kind, gracious teacher, God has given us the "test questions" for the judgment seat of Christ beforehand. It's our job to study these test questions so we can be prepared, and make an "A" on the final exam. Here is a list of some of the main areas in our lives that will be tested when we stand before the Lord:

1. How we treat other believers (Hebrews 6:10; Matthew 10:41–42).
2. How we employ our God-given talents and abilities (Matthew 25:14–29; Luke 19:11–26; 1 Corinthians 12:4; 2 Timothy 1:6; 1 Peter 4:10).
3. How we use our money (Matthew 6:1–4; 1 Timothy 6:17–19).

4. How well we accept mistreatment and injustice (Matthew 5:11–12; Mark 10:29–30; Luke 6:27–28, 35; Romans 8:18; 2 Corinthians 4:17; 1 Peter 4:12–13).

5. How we endure suffering and trials (James 1:12; Revelation 2:10).

6. How we spend our time (Psalm 90:9–12; Ephesians 5:16; Colossians 4:5; 1 Peter 1:17).

7. How we run the particular race God has given us (1 Corinthians 9:24; Philippians 2:16; 3:13-14; Hebrews 12:1).

8. How effectively we control our fleshly appetites (1 Corinthians 9:25–27).

9. How many souls we witness to and win for Christ (Proverbs 11:30; Daniel 12:3; 1 Thessalonians 2:19–20).

10. How much the doctrine of the Rapture means to us (2 Timothy 4:8).

11. How faithful we are to God's Word and God's people (Acts 20:26–28; 2 Timothy 4:1–2; Hebrews 13:17; James 3:1; 1 Peter 5:1–2; 2 John 1:7–8).

12. How hospitable we are to strangers (Matthew 25:35–36; Luke 14:12–14).

13. How faithful we are in our vocation (Colossians 3:22–24).

14. How we use our tongue (Matthew 12:36; James 3:1–12).

Carefully consider this list. Read the verses. Develop and grow in these areas of your life so that when you stand before the Lord someday, you can hear those words, "Well done, good and faithful servant" (Matthew 25:21, NIV).

Chapter 30

WHAT KINDS OF REWARDS WILL GOD GIVE?

The Bible is clear that God is a rewarder. But what form will His rewarding take? According to Scripture, the Lord will honor His people at the judgment seat with three different types of rewards.

GREATER CAPACITY TO REFLECT GOD'S GLORY

First, the Bible indicates that in heaven some will be given a greater capacity and ability to reflect and radiate the glory of the Lord than others: "Those who have insight will shine brightly like the brightness of the expanse of heaven, and those who lead the many to righteousness, like the stars forever and ever" (Daniel 12:3).

We could think of it this way. Together as God's redeemed multitude in heaven we will all be like lights in a magnificent chandelier radiating God's glory. But some of us will be twenty-watt bulbs, some sixty, some seventy-five, and some one hundred. We will all shine, but some more than others.

Another way this is presented in the Bible is by the clothing each believer wears. In heaven, after the judgment seat of Christ and the rewarding of the saints, the next great event will be the marriage of the Lamb to His bride. At that marriage, each believer will be clothed in a garment of his or her own making.

One of the chief concerns of every bride-to-be is what she will wear at her wedding and wedding reception. The bride spends hours looking at dresses, shoes, veils, and all the accessories. The marriage of the Lamb should be no different. Revelation 19:8 reminds us that every believer will be present at the wedding feast dressed in the finest white linen, which the Bible says is the good deeds we have done. "It was given to her to clothe herself in fine linen, bright and clean; for the fine linen is the righteous acts of the saints."

These good deeds are not works we have done to enter heaven. We cannot earn the garments of righteousness that Christ has provided for us by His death on the cross. We are, however, to make ourselves ready for the wedding feast every day by sewing the garment we will wear to the wedding feast. How we are dressed on that day will depend on the life we have lived for Christ. I once heard Lehman Strauss say, "Has it ever occurred to you that at the marriage of the bride to the Lamb, each of us will be wearing the wedding garment of our own making?" Make sure that you will be beautifully attired on that day by living for Christ *today*.

GREATER AUTHORITY AND RESPONSIBILITY

Our Lord will also reward faithfulness in this life by giving greater authority and responsibility in the next life. In the Parable of the Pound, or minas, in Luke 19:11–27, Jesus pictured His leaving the earth and going back to heaven with the image of a nobleman calling together all his servants and giving them each ten minas to invest during his absence. He left them each with the charge, "Do business with this until I come back" (v. 13). The King James Version says, "Occupy till I come."

In the next scene, the nobleman returns after his long absence and calls his servants to account for what they did with their minas. One of the servants used his ten minas to bring a return of ten minas. Jesus applauded his faithfulness, and said, "Well done, good slave, because you have been faithful in a very little thing, you are to be in authority over ten cities" (v. 17). Another slave used his ten minas to make five additional minas. To him Jesus said, "And you are to be over five cities" (v. 19). In the Parable of the Talents, Jesus said the same thing to the faithful slave. "Well done, good and faithful slave; you were faithful in a few things, I will put you in charge of many things, enter into the joy of your Master."

While Jesus didn't give all the details of what this rule over cites entails in the life to come, the overarching principle is clear: Faithful stewardship in this life with the gifts, opportunities, resources, and talents the Lord gives us will bring greater responsibility and authority in the future kingdom of God.

So at least one aspect of reward in the next life entails greater or lesser responsibility and authority based on faithfulness in this life. As someone has said about our lives on earth, "This is training time for reigning time."

CROWNS

Third, the New Testament focuses specifically on five particular crowns or rewards that the faithful will receive at the judgment seat. These crowns are representative of the kinds of conduct and service that will be rewarded by the Lord.

The incorruptible crown (1 Corinthians 9:24–27)

The reward for those who consistently practice self-discipline and self-control over their physical appetites.

The crown of righteousness (2 Timothy 4:8)

The reward for those who eagerly look for the Lord's coming and live a righteous life in view of this fact.

The crown of life (James 1:12; Revelation 2:10)

The sufferer's crown is given to those who faithfully endure and persevere under the trials and tests of life.

The crown of rejoicing (1 Thessalonians 2:19)

This is the soul winner's crown, given to those who win people for Christ.

The crown of glory (1 Peter 5:1–4)

The shepherd's crown will be given to those pastors, elders, and church leaders who lovingly, graciously shepherd and oversee God's people.

CASTING CROWNS

One question that you may be asking at this point is: What will we do with these crowns? Will we wear them around the streets of gold to show off? Will we compare them to the number of crowns others have received? The Bible is clear that having been rewarded by the Lord, the redeemed will immediately give all glory and honor for their rewards back to the Lord.

After receiving these rewards in heaven at the judgment seat, the redeemed will fall down and worship the Lord, lay their crowns at His feet in front of His throne, and sing the praises of His worth and honor. Revelation 4:10–11 says:

The twenty-four elders will fall down before Him who sits on the throne, and will worship Him who lives forever and ever, and will cast their crowns before the throne, saying, "Worthy are You, our Lord and our God, to receive glory and honor and power; for You created all things, and because of Your will they existed, and were created."

The crowns of the redeemed will be cast at the feet of the great Redeemer in humble gratitude to the only One who is worthy of glory, power, and honor.

Chapter 31

WILL EVERY BELIEVER RECEIVE A REWARD IN HEAVEN?

Unless I miss my guess, you have another question about heavenly rewards on the tip of your tongue. Will every believer in Christ receive a reward? Will some of us be left out completely and walk away with an uncrowned head?

I have often heard that many believers will walk away from the judgment seat of Christ totally empty-handed. Some Bible teachers insist that a believer can live his or her entire life and have nothing at the end that is truly rewardable by God. The chief support for this notion is 1 Corinthians 3:13–15, which says:

> Each man's work will become evident; for the day will show it because it is to be revealed with fire, and the fire itself will test the quality of each man's work. If any man's work which he has built on it remains, he will receive a

reward. If any man's work is burned up, he will suffer loss; but he himself will be saved, yet so as through fire.

The context of these verses makes it clear that Paul refers here to the local church at Corinth that he helped found. Paul had laid the foundation there by his preaching of the gospel of Jesus Christ. Jesus was the only and sure foundation for the church. Others had been left there in leadership positions to build the superstructure on the foundation. In their roles as undershepherds, these leaders could choose different kinds of material to use in their building efforts. They could use that which was valuable, enduring, and according to God's wisdom—symbolized by the gold, silver, and precious stones. Or they could use worthless, transitory materials according to man's wisdom—symbolized by the wood, hay, and straw.

The Corinthians' selection of building materials couldn't be more critical—because a day of inspection is coming. Someday, at the judgment seat, Jesus will put their building efforts to the test. Their works will be exposed to the fire of God's scrutiny and examination. The worthwhile materials will come through the fire while the worthless ones will be consumed. First Corinthians 3:14–15 says, "If any man's work which he has built on it remains, he will receive a reward. If any man's work is burned up, he will suffer loss; but he himself will be saved, yet so as through fire."

This passage clearly says that whatever happens to the man's work, he himself will be saved. This supports the biblical doctrine of the eternal security of the believer. Our salvation rests not on our own works, but wholly on the merit of Christ. But does this mean that some will have *all* their works burned up and receive no reward?

Keeping the context in mind (always a cardinal rule in Bible study), these verses focus on church leaders at Corinth, building the church there on the foundation Paul had left behind. It means that those who are in leadership in churches, building a ministry, must be careful what kinds of materials they use to build the church or ministry. They must be careful not to thoughtlessly follow every new trend and method. They must build with what will last. Building carelessly or improperly forfeits reward for that area of life. This passage doesn't say that they get no reward for anything in their entire life, but in the context, refers to their work in building the local assembly. Those who build the church carelessly will lose their reward for that specific part of their life and service.

In fact, just a few verses later, Paul seems to indicate that every believer will receive some reward in heaven. First Corinthians 4:5 says, "Therefore do not go on passing judgment before the time, but wait until the Lord comes who will both bring to light the things hidden in the darkness and disclose the motives of men's hearts; and then *each man's praise* will come to him from God."

The phrase "each man's praise will come to him from God" seems to indicate that each man or woman who appears before Christ at His judgment seat will have something that the Lord can praise—some work, act, deed, or attitude the Lord will commend and reward.

This is just another manifestation of the amazing grace of our Lord.

PART FIVE

Angels
and
the Afterlife

Chapter 32

WHEN CHRISTIANS DIE, DO ANGELS CARRY THEM TO HEAVEN?

In recent years people have become fascinated with angels. Hundreds of books have been written about every aspect of angels. Some have fostered an unhealthy preoccupation with angels, but many have helped people gain a deeper, more accurate understanding of what the Bible says about these powerful servants of God Most High.

The Bible tells us that unfallen angels serve several important functions: They worship and serve God, they execute God's judgment on the wicked, and they war with demons.

In relation to believers, angels carry out many functions as ministering spirits (Hebrews 1:14). Here are a few of the more prominent ones.

1. Guiding (Matthew 1:20–21).
2. Providing (Genesis 21:17–20).

3. Delivering (Acts 5:17–20).
4. Protecting (2 Kings 6:16; Daniel 6:20–23).
5. Answering prayer (Daniel 9:20–24).

But one function of angels that is often completely overlooked is the ministry of angels to believers at the time of death. I believe that the Bible teaches that when a believer dies, angels carry his or her spirit home to heaven. This idea is expressed beautifully in the old spiritual "Swing Low, Sweet Chariot":

Swing low, sweet chariot,
Comin' for to carry me home!

I looked over Jordan and what did I see,
Comin' for to carry me home!
A band of angels comin' after me,
Comin' for to carry me home!

Swing low, sweet chariot,
Comin' for to carry me home!

Where does this idea come from? Is it just wishful thinking, or does the Bible really say anything about it?

In Jesus' parable in Luke 16:19–31, there was a poor beggar named Lazarus whose body was covered with sores that dogs gathered to lick. This poor man sat at the gate of a rich man's estate. Luke 16:22 says that when Lazarus died, he "was carried away by the angels to Abraham's bosom."

What an experience this must have been for poor Lazarus. One moment he was collapsed at the rich man's gate, a dying beggar, and the next moment he was being carried by angels to heaven. In this life his companions were dogs licking his sores, but in death, mighty angels came, swept him into their embrace, and carried him into the presence of the living God.[53]

But Lazarus isn't the only one in the Bible transported to heaven by angels. Scripture also seems to indicate that Jesus Himself was carried or at least escorted by angels when He ascended from the Mount of Olives to glory. Luke 24:51 says, "While He was blessing them, He parted from them." Many ancient manuscripts contain the words "He parted from them and was carried up to heaven." This translation is reflected in the King James Version and the English Standard Version. The New English Translation says, "He went away from them and was taken up into heaven."

Also, Acts 1:9, which records the ascension of Jesus, says, "After he had said these things, He was lifted up while they were looking on, and a cloud received Him out of their sight." Angels appeared immediately to the watching disciples with the promise that Jesus would someday return just as He left. This may indicate that angels had the privilege of carrying the Lord Jesus on His journey back home to heaven (and will also accompany Him on His return!).

In Jude 1:9, we're told that Michael the archangel disputed with Satan over the body of Moses when he died. Moses' body was a concern of Michael's.[54] His spirit may have been as well.

But why would we even *need* angels to carry us to heaven when we die? David Jeremiah, the popular Bible teacher on the *Turning Point* radio program, suggests an excellent explanation:

> One reason may be related to the fact that Satan is described as "the ruler of the kingdom of the air" (Ephesians 2:2). Perhaps we must cross this "kingdom of the air" in going from earth to heaven. Our temporary home here and our permanent home there may be

separated by an immense stretch of enemy territory. It's a trip angels must take often, so it will be a great comfort to have them at our side as we traverse it ourselves.

In *Somewhere Angels,* Larry Libby gives children another reason: "God wants you home so much he'll send his own angel to meet you. And don't be surprised if the angel is wearing a big smile."[55]

In his famous book *Angels: God's Secret Agents,* Billy Graham echoes this same idea:

Death is robbed of much of its terror for the true believer, but we still need God's protection as we take that last journey. At the moment of death the spirit departs from the body and moves through the atmosphere. But the Scripture teaches us that the devil lurks there. He is "the prince of the power of the air" (Ephesians 2:2). If the eyes of our understanding were opened, we would probably see the air filled with demons, the enemies of Christ. If Satan could hinder the angel of Daniel 10 for three weeks on his mission to earth, we can imagine the opposition a Christian may encounter at death. But Christ at Calvary cleared a road through Satan's kingdom. When Christ came to earth, He had to pass through the devil's territory and open up a beachhead here. That is one reason He was accompanied by a host of angels when He came (Luke 2:8–14). And this is why angels will accompany Him when He comes again (Matthew 16:27). Till then, the moment of death is Satan's final opportunity to attack the true believer, but God has sent His angels to guard us at that time.[56]

Billy Graham gives a beautiful summary of what all of this means to you and me:

> Once I stood in London to watch Queen Elizabeth return from an overseas trip. I saw the parade of dignitaries, the marching bands, the crack troops, the waving flags. I saw all the splendor that accompanies the homecoming of a queen. However, that was nothing compared to the homecoming of a true believer who has said goodbye here to all of the suffering of this life and been immediately surrounded by angels who carry him upward to the glorious welcome awaiting the redeemed in heaven.[57]

Chapter 33

DO PEOPLE BECOME ANGELS IN HEAVEN?

As I get older, I find myself taking time each morning to quickly peruse the obituary page in our local newspaper. Several times recently I have noticed statements to the effect that the person who has just died has become one of "God's angels." This seems to be a very common misconception today, especially when a young child dies.

We have all seen the cartoons of a person with wings on his back, strumming a harp, sitting on a cloud, looking down to earth. People seem to be comforted by the thought that their loved ones, especially children who die young, become angels when they get to heaven.

Throughout the Bible the existence of angels is assumed. The creation of angels is referred to in Psalm 148. They were present at the creation of the world and were so filled with wonder and gladness that they "shouted for joy" (Job 38:7).

Angels are created beings. It is evident that they can manifest themselves in human form and at times were mistaken for men. Interestingly (and this also runs contrary to popular depictions), they never appear in female form. At least some ranks of angels do have wings, such as the seraphim described in Isaiah 6:2 (see Revelation 4:8).

Angels and humans are similar in several ways: 1) both are servants of God, 2) both are immortal, i.e., they will live forever, and 3) both have personality (mind, will, and emotions).

But while these similarities exist, the Bible is clear that angels are angels, and humans are humans. We are two totally different orders of beings. While we possess a spirit, we are also creatures of flesh. Angels are not. Angels can assume human appearance and human functions such as eating and drinking (Genesis 18:1–8), but men and women do *not* become angels in heaven.

Once an angel, always and angel. Once a human, always a human.

Support for the idea that people become angels when they die is sometimes drawn from a misunderstanding of the teaching of Jesus in two verses.

"For in the resurrection they neither marry nor are given in marriage, but are like angels in heaven." (Matthew 22:30)

"For when they rise from the dead, they neither marry nor are given in marriage, but are like angels in heaven." (Mark 12:25)

Jesus deals with the subject of marriage in these passages. Angels, wondrous beings that they are, were never given the command to "be fruitful and multiply." They have no marital relationships and no ability to procreate.

Jesus' point in these verses is that in heaven *neither will people*. Our mandate to "be fruitful and multiply" is limited only to this earthly sphere. In heaven, we will be in a different, glorified body that will totally eclipse our present earthly tent. In heaven we will be *like* angels in that one aspect—no more procreation—but we will not *become* angels.

There are at least four points in Scripture that prove believers do not become angels at death. First, despite the general similarities between angels and humans, there are marked differences. Angels are individual creations of God, while humans are a race. When Satan fell, each angel had a choice whether to join in the rebellion, and one-third made that horrific decision (Revelation 12:3). But when Adam, the head of the human race, fell, he took us all with him (Romans 5:12).

Second, the Bible makes it clear that one day God's people—redeemed human beings—will actually judge the angels (1 Corinthians 6:2). In this present life we are a little lower than the angels, but in the life to come we will be over them (Psalm 8:5; Hebrews 2:7). If we will judge the angels, then we must be different from angels. It's only logical.

Third, according to Luke 16:22 angels came and carried the poor man's soul to paradise, to the bosom of Abraham. If we become angels, why would we need angels to come carry us to the presence of the Lord?

Fourth, several New Testament passages distinguish between redeemed people and angels in heaven. Here are two examples.

> But you have come to Mount Zion and to the city of the living God, the heavenly Jerusalem, and to myriads of angels, to the general assembly and church of the firstborn who are enrolled in heaven, and to God, the Judge of all, and to the spirits of righteous made perfect, and

to Jesus, the mediator of a new covenant, and to the sprinkled blood, which speaks better than the blood of Abel. (Hebrews 12:22–24)

This passage lists all the inhabitants of heaven. Notice that angels and the church of the firstborn (believers in the present church age) are distinct from each other:

Then I looked, and I heard the voice of many angels around the throne and the living creatures and the elders; and the number of them was myriads of myriads, and thousands of thousands. (Revelation 5:11)

The "elders" is a reference to the twenty-four elders mentioned twelve times in the book of Revelation. I believe these elders are symbolic of the church of Jesus Christ in heaven. And the angels in heaven and these elders are mentioned separately, indicating that they aren't the same.

So, if you were hoping to become an angel in heaven, then I'm sorry to disappoint you. But actually, it shouldn't be a disappointment at all. Because according to the Scripture our place in heaven will be above the angels. We are the bride of Christ. For eternity, we will be second only to God in the order and authority of His unshakable Kingdom.

What a destiny awaits us!

PART SIX

Everyday
Life in
Heaven

Chapter 34

WILL WE KNOW EACH OTHER IN HEAVEN?

Almost every person has probably asked this question at one time or another. Our hearts long to know if we will recognize our friends and loved ones in heaven, and if they will know us. Interestingly, in a recent survey, less than 50 percent of the respondents believed they would see friends, relatives, or their spouses in heaven.

Well, I've got good news for you—we will not only see our friends and loved ones in heaven; we will know them. In fact, we won't really know each other *until* we get to heaven. Only in heaven, when all the masks and facades are torn away, will we really know one another and enjoy intimate, unhindered fellowship.

Luke 16:19–31 offers strong evidence that we will recognize each other in heaven. In that parable, the rich man recognizes Lazarus in heaven and remembers all the facts about their relationship on earth. The rich man even remembers his five brothers who are still on earth.

For that matter, Scripture indicates we will even recognize people we never met here on earth!

At the Transfiguration of Jesus, Peter knew that the two men with Jesus were Elijah and Moses (Matthew 17:1–4). Obviously, Peter had never met Moses and Elijah. How did he know who they were? It appears that he had an intuitive knowledge that enabled him to know immediately who they were. I believe that it will be the same way in heaven. All of the Lord's people will possess this intuitive knowledge that will enable us to recognize our friends and loved ones as well as the redeemed of all the ages.

We will never meet a stranger in heaven!

Chapter 35

WILL WE
KNOW EVERYTHING
IN HEAVEN?

When someone dies, I've often heard people say, *"Well, all of his questions have been answered."*

I know what people mean by this.

They mean that in heaven we will know and understand so much more than we ever knew and understood on earth. Certainly this must be so. But we won't know everything! Knowing everything would make us omniscient (all knowing), which is only true of God. Only the infinite can know everything.

When we get to heaven, both our minds and bodies will be glorified and perfected, but we will still be human; we will still be finite beings. Clearly, our capacity for learning will be exponentially enhanced (1 Corinthians 13:12). Nevertheless, our knowledge will always be limited and finite.

As God's children, I believe we will spend eternity learning more and more (and more) about God and His ways. But God will always be infinite, and we will always be finite. Angels in heaven, who are perfect creatures, don't know everything. They are constantly learning about God and His ways (1 Peter 1:12). For all eternity we will always be learning and discovering more about the wonders and majesty of our Great God and His creation.

Peter Kreeft makes this interesting observation:

> When you come to think of it, knowing everything would be more like Hell than Heaven for us. For one thing, we need progress and hope: we need to look forward to knowing something new tomorrow. Mystery is our mind's food.... Only omnipotence can bear the burden of omniscience; only God's shoulders are strong enough to carry the burden of infinite knowledge without losing the joy.[58]

We will never know everything, but we will know and learn things we never imagined here on earth. We will learn the answers to our deepest questions and answers to questions we never even thought to ask.

I don't know about you, but I'm looking forward to that.

Chapter 36

WHAT WILL WE DO IN HEAVEN?

This frequently asked question takes on many different forms.

"Will there be football in heaven?"

"Will I be able to golf in heaven?"

"Will I sit around all day on a cloud strumming a harp?"

Most people seem to view heaven as a place of inactivity and endless boredom. In a poem Rudyard Kipling wrote,

When earth's last picture is painted
    and the tubes are twisted and dried;
When the oldest colors have faded
    and the youngest critic has died;
We shall rest, and faith, we shall need it,
    lay down for an eon or two,
Till the Master of all good workmen
    shall put us to work anew.

This is a kind of Rip van Winkle view of heaven.

Children have their own perspectives on heaven. Here is how a few children responded to the question, "What do you do in heaven?"

"You can do anything you want, silly!"

"You can eat candy, and don't get fat or cavities."

"You water-skate all day long!" declared one squirmy first grader. When asked, "What's water-skating?" She smiled shyly and replied, *"You'll find out."*

"You can stay up all day and all night, and your parents can't make you go to bed because there aren't any—beds. There are parents."

"You help people on earth be smarter."

"Your play the harp all day, whether you like it or not."

"You have to paint clouds."

"Most of the time you try to get dry because it seems like it's always raining in heaven."[59]

Before we consider what we will do in heaven, I believe it is important to see at least a little bit of what we won't do in heaven.

Think about it. We will never sin, never make mistakes, never need to confess, never have to repair or replace things (no leaky faucets, no changing lightbulbs, no car repairs). We will never have to help others, defend ourselves, apologize, experience guilt, battle with Satan or demons, share the gospel of Jesus Christ, or experience healing, rehabilitation, loneliness, depression, or fatigue.

While the Bible doesn't tell us as much as we would like to know about what we will do in heaven, it does focus on at least six primary activities. These six things provide us with a general overview, a basic job description, of what we will do.

It is estimated that there are forty thousand different occupations in the United States. Only a small percentage of workers are very satisfied with their responsibilities. There are personnel problems, lack of adequate pay, wearisome hours of routine tasks, and so on. But all of these problems will be gone forever in heaven as each of us fulfills our assigned responsibilities.

Let's look briefly at the six primary activities the Lord has for us in our Father's house. While I'm sure these six activities do not exhaust the infinite activities the Lord has for us, they do serve as a basic overview of the kinds of things the Lord has in store.

1. Singing and praising God (Revelation 4:10–11; 7:7–12; 11:15–17; 14:3; 15:2–4; 19:4–6)

Robert E. Coleman relates this beautiful story.

> In some of the medieval monasteries following the custom in the temple of Israel, it was a rule that hymns of praise to God would never cease. When one of the monks would stop singing, another would pick up the song. Thus, day and night, the joyous sound was heard.
>
> On one occasion a monastery was overrun by a band of Norse raiders. They slaughtered the monks without mercy, including the one who was singing. However, one monk was able to escape and hide in an inaccessible spot, where the attackers were not likely to find him. But when he heard the songs of praise cease, instinctively he took it up, thus betraying his place of refuge.[60]

Heaven is like that. It is a place of uninhibited joy and spontaneous, unending worship. Even those who can't carry a tune in a bucket here on earth will be able to sing rapturously in heaven. Of course, there will be many songs we *won't* sing in heaven, such as "When We All Get to Heaven" or "Sweet Hour of Prayer." But I'm sure we will still sing "Great Is Thy Faithfulness," "All Hail the Power of Jesus' Name," and "O Worship the King."

Heaven is a place of singing praises to the Lamb and to the great Name of the One who sits on the throne.

2. Serving (Revelation 1:6; 7:15; 19:5; 22:3)

The Bible says clearly that we will serve the Lord forever, but it never tells us specifically how we will serve. All we know for certain is that we will serve as believer-priests forever in God's presence.

3. Supervising (Matthew 25:21; Luke 19:17–19; 1 Corinthians 6:3; 2 Timothy 2:12; Revelation 3:20–21; 20:4; 22:5)

God's people will reign forever with the Lord over the new heaven and new earth as servant-kings. We will judge the angels. Again, there are no specifics as to how this will be carried out. We will have to wait until heaven to get the specific job description.

4. Sharing (1 John 3:2; Revelation 22:4)

Have you ever wondered what it would be like to be a member of a perfect church? We will find out in heaven. The fellowship in heaven will be sweet—first with our precious Lord as we share intimate communion with Him, and then with one another.

In *Pilgrim's Progress,* Christian is asked why he has such a strong desire to go to heaven. He responds, "Why, there I hope to see him alive, that did hang dead on the Cross; and there I hope to be rid of all those things that to this day are in me an annoyance to me; there they say there is no death, and there I shall dwell with such company as I like best." Christian desired to go to heaven to be with Christ, to see the One who died for him, and to enjoy the good company of fellow believers.

In the song "My Savior First of All," nineteenth-century hymn writer Fanny Crosby wrote:

When my life work is ended, and I cross the swelling tide,
When the bright and glorious morning I shall see,
I shall know my Redeemer when I reach the other side,
And His smile will be the first to welcome me....

Thru the gates of the city in a robe of spotless white,
He will lead me where no tears will ever fall;
In the glad songs of ages I shall mingle with delight
But I long to meet my Savior first of all.

Those words had a special significance because Fanny Crosby was born blind. When she died, the first person she saw was Jesus Christ. What will our relationship be with the Lord in heaven? We will see Him and be with Him. That will be our ultimate satisfaction.

5. Studying (1 Corinthians 13:12)

Since, as we have seen, we will never know everything, we will spend eternity learning more about the infinite majesty of God's person and ways.

6. Being served (Luke 12:35–37)

In heaven there is no mention of believers serving each other, only of us serving God and Him serving us. Luke 12:35–37 says the Lord of Glory when He comes "will gird himself to serve, and have them recline at the table, and will come up and wait on them."

Ever the servant, the Lord Jesus will minister to His people and meet our needs forever.

Chapter 37

WILL HEAVEN BE BORING?

For some reason many people have the idea that since heaven will be a perfect place, it will be a perfectly *boring* place.

Just think about it. What if every time you went golfing you made eighteen holes in one? Well, if you have ever seen me play golf, you know that I would never get tired of that.

Or some people think of heaven as similar to a church service here on earth. Except it goes on forever. That doesn't sound too enticing.

But that's not what heaven will be like. Heaven, as we have seen, will be a place of constant development, growth, service, learning, and exploring.

We will be constantly learning more and more about our infinite God, about His glorious creation, and about one another, as we live in a rich, unhindered fellowship unlike anything we have ever imagined on earth.

Peter Kreeft, a professor of philosophy from Boston College, says it well:

> Why won't we get bored in heaven? Because we are with God, and God is infinite. We never come to the end of exploring Him. He is new every day. Because we are with God, and God is eternal. Time does not pass (a condition for boredom); it just is.... Because we are with God, and God is love. Even on earth, the only people who are never bored are lovers.[61]

Make no mistake. Heaven will be perfect, but it will never be boring. It will challenge and exhilarate us every moment. And it will never end.

Chapter 38

CAN PEOPLE IN HEAVEN SEE WHAT'S HAPPENING ON EARTH?

This is a question that every believer has probably asked at one time or another. We are curious about what we will know and be able to see when we get to heaven and whether our loved ones in heaven right now can look down and observe what we're doing on earth.

The Bible never answers this question clearly, but it does give some hints that people in heaven can see some of what is transpiring on earth. The main passage that is used to support this idea is Hebrews 12:1. Following the inspiring list of the faithful from the past such as Enoch, Abraham, and Moses, the writer to the Hebrews concludes, "Therefore, since we have so great a cloud of witnesses surrounding us, let us also lay aside every encumbrance and the sin which so easily entangles us, and let us run with endurance the race that is set before us."

You may have heard this huge cloud of witnesses described as an audience in a huge heavenly stadium watching us here on earth. They are like the crowd in the stands at the Super Bowl, looking down at those of us on the playing field of life as we run the particular race in life that God has given us to run.

Nevertheless, the real motivation in this passage is not that they see us, but that we see them! As we look back on the patient endurance and faithfulness in their earthly journeys, we find ourselves longing to emulate their lives. Abel. Noah. Abraham. Rahab. Moses. David. They are witnesses to us of God's approval of the life of faith.

But in other places the Bible does reveal that people in heaven are aware of at least some events that transpire on the earth. For instance, Samuel the prophet, after his death, appeared to King Saul and was aware of at least some of the events surrounding Saul and his kingdom (1 Samuel 28:16–18). The rejoicing in heaven over the salvation of a sinner on earth seems to include believers already in heaven as well as angels (Luke 15:7, 10). The martyrs in heaven in Revelation 6:9–10 are aware that their persecutors are still alive on earth. The multitude in heaven in Revelation 19:1–6 is aware of the destruction of Babylon on earth.

The Bible declines to give us any specific details as to whether God will limit our knowledge of events on earth or whether we'll know everything that transpires. Some people often question why God would allow those in heaven to look down and see all the sin, sorrow, and misery in this world. This might take a lot of the happiness out of heaven.

Even so, Scriptures tell us that those who are in heaven know at least some of what is happening on this earth and follow these events with intense interest.

However, it is also safe to say that once we get to heaven we may not be as interested in watching the events on earth as we might think. In Revelation 4–5, the church in heaven is pictured by the twenty-four elders falling down and worshiping the Lord.

While believers in heaven certainly know at least some of the main events occurring on earth, it is clear from Revelation that when we get to heaven we will primarily be consumed with worshiping the Lamb on the throne, not looking back over our shoulders at a troubled planet.

Chapter 39

HOW CAN CHRISTIANS ENJOY HEAVEN KNOWING THAT PEOPLE ARE IN HELL?

I must confess I have asked this myself many times.

It is a difficult question. After all, we know that heaven is a place of joy, happiness, delight, and lightness of heart. Revelation 21:4 says that the Lord "will wipe away every tear from their eyes." Heaven will be a place with no tears, sorrow, or crying. Yet how can we experience no sorrow for those we know who are in hell?

One solution to this apparent dilemma is to conclude that in heaven the Lord will purge our memory of our lost loved ones and friends and the existence of hell. Several verses have been used to support this position: Deuteronomy 25:19; Psalm 9:5; 69:28; 109:13.

We might draw our main support for this view from Isaiah 65:17–19:

"For behold, I create new heavens and a new earth; and the former things will not be remembered or come to mind. But be glad and rejoice forever in what I create; for behold, I create Jerusalem for rejoicing and her people for gladness. I will also rejoice in Jerusalem and be glad in My people; and there will no longer be heard in her the voice of weeping and the sound of crying."

While these verses could support this idea, the main point appears to be that in our future state, everything will be so wonderful that we will forget the sorrows and weeping of this life. Our focus will be on the joy and gladness of God's new creation.

To say that believers in heaven will no longer remember people they knew on earth—or that hell even exists—is to say that in heaven we will know less than we knew here on earth. And yet the Bible would seem to say that we will know more in heaven, not less.

The best solution to the problem is to recognize that in heaven we will have a perfected spirit with an ability to see things clearly from the divine perspective. In heaven, believers will know about hell and will know that people we love are there, but we will also be in the presence of the Holy God and will know that those who rejected Him do not deserve to be in His presence. For the first time in our lives we fully see sin in the light of His holiness and will understand the extent of what it means for the lost to be Christ-rejecting enemies of God who spurned His gracious offer of salvation.

We will also know that we do not deserve to be in His presence either. We will more clearly understand both His undiminished justice and holiness and His undeserved grace and mercy. And recognizing the holiness and grace of God, we will unendingly thank Him for our salvation and understand (at least in some measure) His righteous, eternal punishment of the lost.

Chapter 40

IS THERE TIME
IN HEAVEN?

Here on this earth we are time-bound creatures. The clock is always there. We show up for work on time and end at quitting time. We make appointments. Events have specific starting times. We carry watches, have clocks in our cars and clocks on our cell phones. Time is everywhere. We are always asking, "What time is it?" Time is an essential part of life.

But will heaven be different? Will time as we know it be a part of life in heaven? First, we need to understand what "time" really means. According to *Webster's New Collegiate Dictionary,* time is the duration or "measured period during which an action, process, or condition exists or continues." Time involves seeing things in succession.

The Bible speaks of a God who is timeless, a God who is not bound by viewing events in succession. God transcends time and all temporal limitations. He sees and knows the end from the beginning. God knows and sees things instantaneously and simultaneously. In Genesis 1:1, God created time as we know it: "In the beginning." So, while God transcends time, He created time and works in it with His creation.

Does this mean that in heaven there will be no time? Not necessarily. The Bible seems to indicate that even in heaven people see things occurring in succession—to some extent at least—and are aware of the passage of time. In Revelation 6:10 some martyred believers in heaven are crying out to God in loud voices, saying, "How long, O Lord, holy and true, will You refrain from judging and avenging our blood on those who dwell on the earth?"

These saints in heaven still have some concept of time. They ask God, "How long?"

Revelation 8:1 also indicates some concept of measured duration of events in heaven. The apostle John wrote, "When the Lamb broke the seventh seal, there was silence in heaven for about half an hour." Of course, this could be speaking of the passage of time from John's frame of reference on earth as he saw the glorious vision of the blowing of the heavenly trumpets. But it seems to me that it refers to the passage of time in heaven.

Many things—indeed, *most* things—will be very different in heaven than here on earth. But one thing that apparently will remain from this earth is the presence of time in some form.

Chapter 41

WILL THERE BE MARRIAGE IN HEAVEN?

Those who have experienced a long relationship with a spouse they love and cherish often want to know if that relationship will continue after physical death. For many happily married couples, it is hard to imagine life without that special relationship to their spouse.

In the book of Matthew, however, Jesus clearly stated that marriage as we know it here on earth will not carry over to the hereafter. "For in the resurrection they neither marry nor are given in marriage, but are like angels in heaven (22:30).

Two other New Testament passages, Romans 7:1–3 and 1 Corinthians 7:39, also state that marriage as a physical union is terminated at the death of either spouse. I've performed dozens of weddings in my years as a pastor, and the final line of the declaration of intent for the couple is "till death do you part." Even the wedding vows recognize the fact that marriage terminates at death.

But what does this really mean? That married couples who were soul mates on earth will no longer share a special relationship in heaven? I don't think so. Couples who shared the closest intimacy on earth will continue to know, treasure, and appreciate each other in the life of the Lord forever.

I plan to spend all of eternity with my wife, Cheryl, in a relationship that goes far beyond anything we have experienced here on earth. No, we won't be married to each other, in that old, earthly sense. But we will both be part of the bride of the Lord Jesus Christ. We will be married to the heavenly Bridegroom. In no way, however, will this preclude Cheryl and me from enjoying an ever-deepening, wonderful, unique relationship.

Forever.

Chapter 42

IS THERE SEX
IN HEAVEN?

I read a story about a man whose wife sent him to a counselor because she thought he was too focused on sex. When the man sat down with the counselor, he said, "I'm going to show you some pictures, and I want you to tell me the first word that comes into your mind." The counselor held up a picture of a tree, and the man said, "Sex." He then held up a picture of a beautiful lake, and the man again said, "Sex." This happened again and again with many pictures.

Finally, the counselor put the pictures on the table and said, "Is sex the only thing you ever think about?"

"Hey, don't get mad at me," the man responded. "You're the one with all the dirty pictures."

This reminds me of our society. We see sex everywhere we look. We live in a sex-saturated society. Sex fills our television shows, movies, novels, computers, billboards, and gossip columns.

So it shouldn't surprise us that people today are interested in the question of sex in heaven.

It's interesting to me how many people wonder about this issue. No one has ever asked me this question in a public Q & A session, but I've been asked privately many times. Always by men.

And what is the answer to this touchy question about sex in heaven? Yes and no.

That isn't a cop-out or a dodge. The reason for this double answer is that sex is both something *we are* and something *we do*. We need to consider each of these issues separately.

First, sex is what we are in essence or nature—that is, male and female. How often have you filled out a form or questionnaire that had a blank to fill in asking for your gender? Sex—our maleness or femaleness—is part of the essence of our being. God created this distinction of the sexes in the Garden of Eden. He created them male and female (Genesis 1:27). It is likely that in heaven those who were males on earth will always be males, and females will be females. Daniel will still be Daniel, and Esther will still be Esther. God will not *remove* our sexual nature, but will *redeem* it.

Second, sex is also an act that is performed between husbands and wives for pleasure and procreation. It is doubtful that sex as a physical act will be present in heaven. Sex is an act of intimacy and pleasure reserved for married couples. Since there will be no marriage in heaven or need for procreation, the act of sex will not persist as an expression of love. As we noted in the last question, we will be like angels in heaven in the sense of not being married, procreating, or sharing sexual intimacy (Matthew 22:30).

In heaven (believe it or not), there will undoubtedly be something far greater to enjoy than sexual intercourse. Men and women will enjoy each other in a much deeper way than can be accomplished by physical sex. As Hank Hanegraaf writes:

Thus, we can rest assured that our temporary earthly passions are but a pale shadow of the pleasure we will experience in heaven when symbol is supplanted by substance.... In heaven, pleasure that the male and female sex will experience in one another will be infinitely magnified because in eternity our earthly conception of sex will have been eclipsed.[62]

Peter Kreeft provides an excellent illustration of this point:

I think there will probably be millions of more adequate ways to express love than the clumsy ecstasy of fitting two bodies together like pieces of a jigsaw puzzle. Even the most satisfying earthly intercourse between spouses cannot perfectly express *all* their love. If the possibility of intercourse in Heaven is not actualized, it is only for the same reason that lovers do not eat candy during intercourse; there is something much better to do. The question of intercourse in Heaven is like the child's question whether you can eat candy during intercourse: a funny question only from the adult's point of view. Candy is one of children's greatest pleasures; how can they conceive of a pleasure so intense that is renders candy irrelevant? Only if you know both can you compare two things, and all those who have tasted both the delights of physical intercourse with the earthly beloved and the delights of spiritual intercourse with God testify that there is simply no comparison.[63]

As Psalm 16:11 reminds us, "In Your presence is fullness of joy; in Your right hand there are pleasures forever."

So, will there be sex in heaven?

Again, *yes* and *no*. Yes, in the sense of who we are, but no, in the sense of the physical act.

Chapter 43

DO PEOPLE IN HEAVEN WEAR CLOTHES?

Who thinks up these questions? You may not have ever thought about this before, but I've been asked this question more than once.

In the original creation of Adam and Eve in the Garden of Eden, they were "both naked and were not ashamed" (Genesis 2:25). When sin entered the world by their rebellion, they sensed their guilt before God and covered themselves. From that time on people have worn clothes. But since heaven is perfect—a place of no sin or corruption—why would people there wear clothes?

The Bible indicates that in heaven Christ, people, and angels all have some form of covering or clothing.

When the church of Jesus Christ is pictured as His glorious bride, she is clothed. "It was given to her to clothe herself in fine linen, bright and clean; for the fine linen is the righteous acts of the saints" (Revelation 19:8). White clothing is a heavenly reward for the overcomer in Revelation 3:5. Also, the multitude of martyred saints in heaven in Revelation 7:9 are "clothed in white robes, and palm branches were in their hands."

Angels too are often described as clothed in linen and sometimes wearing a belt (Daniel 10:5).

The resurrected, glorified Christ is presented in Revelation 1:13 as "clothed in a robe reaching to the feet, and girded across His chest with a golden sash" (see Matthew 17:2). When Jesus comes back to earth to destroy the Antichrist and establish His kingdom, Revelation 19:13 says, "He is clothed with a robe dipped in blood." Believers from heaven who follow Jesus in His conquest are also clothed. "And the armies which are in heaven, clothed in fine linen, white and clean, were following Him on white horses" (19:14).

What exactly this covering will be is not spelled out in the Bible. But it seems clear that in heaven God's people will wear clothing that reflects our righteous standing before a holy God.

Chapter 44

WILL WE EAT
IN HEAVEN?

Eating is such an integral part of our everyday lives on earth that it's natural for us to wonder if we will eat in heaven.

I believe the Bible indicates that we will eat in heaven.

And the best thing about it is we will never get fat.

Jesus, in His glorified body, ate food (Luke 24:41–43). The thousand-year reign of Christ on earth after his Second Coming is often pictured as a great banquet or marriage supper (Matthew 8:11; Revelation 19:9). Also, Revelation 22:1–2 describes the tree of life that will be in the heavenly city:

> "Then he showed me a river of the water of life, clear as crystal, coming from the throne of God and of the Lamb, in the middle of its street. On either side of the river was the tree of life, bearing twelve kinds of fruit, yielding its fruit every month; and the leaves of the tree were for the healing of the nations."

Revelation 22:2 never says specifically that we will eat of the fruit of the tree, but the implication is that this is what the fruit is for. Adam and Eve ate of the fruit from the tree of life in the Garden of Eden (Genesis 3:22).

Some believe that eating in heaven will be something that is possible for us, but not necessary. Something that will be available to us simply for enjoyment and fellowship. Those who hold this view believe that our bodies will be adaptive to food but not dependent on it for survival like they are now.

Others maintain that eating the fruit of the tree of life will be necessary. They hold that the fruit of the tree of life is what will give us immortality, just as it did for Adam and Eve originally.[64]

Whichever of these ideas is correct, the truth remains that we will eat in heaven. In fact, both of these views are probably correct. It will be necessary for us to eat of the tree of life, but we will be able to eat from all kinds of other sources for enjoyment and satisfaction.

The focus in heaven, however, will not be on food and eating, but on our Savior, Jesus Christ, the Bread of Life, who will satisfy our every longing.

Chapter 45

WILL JESUS STILL HAVE SCARS IN HEAVEN?

The Bible teaches that the resurrected, glorified body of Jesus will bear the scars of Calvary forever. When Jesus appeared to His disciples one week after His resurrection, He spoke these words to doubting Thomas: "Reach here with your finger, and see My hands; and reach here your hand and put it into My side; and do not be unbelieving, but believing" (John 20:27).

Jesus still bore the nail scars in His loving hands and the spear scar in His wounded side.

But why would God do this? Why will Jesus bear these scars forever? There are two main reasons. First, to remind Israel of the scarred body of her Messiah. At His second coming to earth, the Jews on earth who have survived the Tribulation will see their wounded Messiah and turn to Him in deep repentance.

"I will pour out on the house of David and on the inhabitants of Jerusalem, the Spirit of grace and of supplication, so that they will look on Me whom they have pierced; and they will mourn for Him, as one mourns for an only son, and they will weep bitterly over Him, like the bitter weeping of a firstborn." (Zechariah 12:10; see also Revelation 1:7)

The scarred body of Jesus will fulfill Bible prophecy when the Jews see Him and repent.

Second, the scars of Jesus will be an eternal reminder to you and me and all the redeemed of the infinite price paid to purchase pardon from our sins. Of all the titles for Jesus in Revelation, the most commonly used is "Lamb" (twenty-eight times). God never wants us to forget His slain Lamb who shed His precious blood for our sins (Revelation 5:6).

I don't know if you've ever thought about this before, but the only man-made thing in heaven will be the scars of Jesus.

Jesus' scars will serve of a constant reminder of what man did to the Son of God, but also what the Son of God did for man.

Chapter 46

WILL WE SEE
GOD IN HEAVEN?

When I was a young boy, I remember asking a noted guest speaker at our church after one of the services if he thought we would actually see God the Father in heaven. He told me that we would see Jesus, who, of course, is God, but that we would not see the Father because He is spirit.

The answer seemed okay, but for some reason I was never really sure that he was correct. Something inside told me that I *would* someday see my heavenly Father—but I didn't have any idea if the Bible supported my impression.

What I didn't realize at that time was that all the Lord's people long to see Him. As the psalmist says, "As the deer pants for the water brooks, so my soul pants for You, O God. My soul thirsts for God, for the living God; when shall I come and appear before God?" (Psalm 42:1–2). The psalmist wanted to see God.

Speaking for all the disciples, Philip said to Jesus, "Show us the Father" (John 14:8).

As I grew older I discovered three key passages that confirm that we will see the manifestation of God (the Father) in heaven, as well as God the Son:

"Blessed are the pure in heart, for they shall see God." (Matthew 5:8)

Immediately I was in the Spirit; and behold, a throne was standing in heaven, and One sitting on the throne. And He who was sitting was like a jasper stone and a sardius in appearance; and there was a rainbow around the throne, like an emerald in appearance. (Revelation 4:2–3)

The One who sits on the throne in Revelation 4–5 is not Jesus, but God the Father. In Revelation 5:13 the One who sits on the throne (God the Father) is clearly distinguished from the Lamb (God the Son).

They will see His face, and His name will be on their foreheads. (Revelation 22:4)

Proponents of the opposite view, however, point to three passages that seem to prove that even believers in Christ will never see God in heaven.

In Exodus 33:20, God declared to Moses, "You cannot see My face, for no man can see Me and live!"

In the first chapter of John's Gospel, the apostle tells us: "No one has seen God at any time; the only begotten God who is in the bosom of the Father, He has explained Him" (v. 18).

Over in 1 Timothy 6:15–16, Paul speaks of "He who is the blessed and only Sovereign, the King of kings and Lord of lords, who alone possesses immortality and dwells in unapproachable light, whom no man has seen or can see. To Him be honor and eternal dominion! Amen."

So how do we reconcile these seemingly contradictory biblical statements? *We will see God...yet no man can see God and live.* How can that be? I believe the three verses above are telling us that man cannot look upon God and live in these earthly human bodies on this side of heaven. In his present state, in his unperfected, unglorified condition, he cannot behold the manifestation of God and survive the experience.

One day soon, however, we will live and move in new, immortal, imperishable bodies fit for heaven. And with new eyes in that glorious place beyond our finite imaginations, we will be granted the inestimable privilege of seeing the localized manifestation of our heavenly Father.

We will see the Father in heaven!

John MacArthur supports this view:

> But I believe that in heaven we will see God Himself with our physical eyes.... God will reveal the light of His glory, and through perfect eyes we will see the very face of God. God is spirit (John 4:24), and spirit is invisible; therefore, whenever God manifests Himself He does so in the form of light.... Seeing Christ and the Father will eternally awe us.[65]

The fact that we will see the Father and the Son in heaven does not mean that there is more than one God. The true God is one (Deuteronomy 6:4). He is one in essence or nature, yet three in person. Another way to put it is that God is one "what" (one essence) and three "whos" (three persons—Father, Son, and Holy Spirit).

We will see the manifestation of the Father in heaven as well as the face of our blessed Savior. "They will see His face, and His name will be on their foreheads" (Revelation 22:4; see 1 Corinthians 13:12).

PART SEVEN

The Ultimate
Extreme Makeover

Chapter 47

WHAT KIND OF BODY WILL WE HAVE IN HEAVEN?

At this writing, so-called reality TV has taken the screen by storm. First, it was *Survivor*. Then more *Survivor*. And more. Then a whole array of shows with every kind of bizarre theme imaginable.

One of the more interesting reality shows to hit the screen is called *Extreme Makeover*.

On this program people with various physical imperfections get the ultimate extreme makeover. They get plastic surgery on one or more places. People want smaller noses, squarer jawlines, more hair, larger breasts, straighter, whiter teeth, and more sumptuous lips. They get liposuction, new hairdos, new clothes, and new shoes. Then at the end of the show they make their grand entrance into a room of anxious family members and friends waiting to see the unveiling of the new, improved version.

Very few people will ever have an extreme makeover in this life. But every believer in Jesus Christ will get a complete overhaul someday.

We all look forward to getting a new body in heaven. This is especially true of those who suffer from one or more of "the five B's of old age": baldness, bifocals, bridges, bulges, and bunions. All of us come to a point in life when we look in the mirror and say, "Mirror, mirror on the wall…you've got to be kidding!"

I read not long ago of an elderly man who looked down and was admiring his new alligator shoes and then suddenly realized he was barefoot.

Someone has described the three stages of life like this: youth, middle age, and you're looking good.

Let's face it. As our outer man begins to fall apart, we begin to groan for glory. We eagerly anticipate our new, remodeled, perfect body in heaven. As 2 Corinthians 5:1–2 tells us,

> For we know that if the earthly tent which is our house
> is torn down, we have a building from God, a house not
> made with hands, eternal in the heavens. For indeed in
> this house we groan, longing to be clothed with our
> dwelling from heaven.

But when we begin to think about our future resurrection bodies, we often have more questions than answers. While the Bible doesn't satisfy our curiosity about every detail, it does give us a basic idea of what our new, glorified bodies will be like.

Generally, we know that our new bodies will be like the resurrected, glorified body of Jesus.

> For our citizenship is in heaven, from which also we
> eagerly wait for a Savior, the Lord Jesus Christ; who will

transform the body of our humble state into conformity with the body of His glory, by the exertion of the power that He has even to subject all things to Himself. (Philippians 3:20–21)

Beloved, now we are children of God, and it has not appeared as yet what we will be. We know that when He appears, we will be like Him, because we will see Him just as He is. (1 John 3:2)

What was Christ's resurrection body like?

- He possessed flesh and bones (Luke 24:39–40).
- He ate food (Luke 24:41–43; John 21:12–15).
- He was recognized by His disciples (Luke 24:31).
- He was not subject to normal laws of time and space. On two separate occasions, Jesus came right through the walls of the room where the disciples were meeting (Luke 24:36; John 20:19, 26). On another occasion He vanished from sight (Luke 24:31).

Our future bodies will be just like the resurrection body of Jesus, and we will be able to do the same things He did in His body.

Joni Eareckson Tada, rendered quadriplegic by a tragic diving accident as a teenager, clings to the hope of one day receiving an eternal resurrected body, like the body of Jesus:

Somewhere in my broken, paralyzed body is the seed of what I shall become. The paralysis makes what I am become all the more grand when you contrast atrophied, useless legs against splendorous resurrected legs. I'm convinced that if there are mirrors in heaven (and why not?), the image I'll see will be unmistakable "Joni," although a much better, brighter Joni. So much so that it's not worth comparing.... I will bear the likeness of Jesus, the man from heaven.[66]

Specifically, the Bible gives several key facts about our future bodies in 1 Corinthians 15:35, 42–49:

But someone will say, "How are the dead raised? And with what kind of body do they come?"... So also is the resurrection of the dead. It is sown a perishable body, it is raised an imperishable body; it is sown in dishonor, it is raised in glory; it is sown in weakness, it is raised in power; it is sown a natural body, it is raised a spiritual body. If there is a natural body, there is also a spiritual body. So also it is written, "The first man, Adam, became a living soul." The last Adam became a life-giving spirit. However, the spiritual is not first, but the natural; then the spiritual. The first man is from the earth, earthy; the second man is from heaven. As is the earthy, so also are those who are earthy; and as is the heavenly, so also are those who are heavenly. Just as we have borne the image of the earthy, we will also bear the image of the heavenly.

EIGHT FABULOUS FACTS
ABOUT OUR FUTURE BODIES

1. They will never be subject to disease, decay, or death. They will be imperishable. Our present bodies are born with an expiration date. Our future bodies will never wear out.

2. They will be perfectly suitable to our new environment. They will be "heavenly" bodies.

3. They will each be unique and diverse from one another. Just as different stars and planets are unique and have varying degrees of glory, we will each maintain a uniqueness and diversity in heaven.

4. They will be vastly superior to our present bodies. As superior as celestial bodies in the heavens are to our little planet earth.

5. They will be glorious—"full of glory." They will never disappoint us.

6. They will be powerful. The future body will be an invincible fortress. We will be like Superman or Wonder Woman without the spandex and tights. Our new body will never get tired, never wear out, and never yield to sin.

7. They will be spiritual, not natural. This doesn't mean they won't be real or physical. It simply means that our new body will allow us to fully express our spiritual nature. Unlike our present natural body, our future body will be unaffected by the physical laws of gravity and space.

   Think of it like this. Consider a book with a sheet of white paper stuck inside it. In this illustration the book is a man's body and the paper sheet is his spirit.

Down here the book controls the spirit. It has the final say. That is the natural body, governed by the physical laws of gravity and space. But now take the white sheet out of the book and wrap it around the book like a cover. Now the sheet (spirit) is on top. It has the final say. This is the spiritual body, unaffected by the physical laws, but able to fully enjoy the blessings of eternity.[67]

8. They will have continuity with our present body, yet be vastly changed. In 1 Corinthians 15, Paul used the picture of planting a seed to represent the placing of a body in the ground at death. When you plant a seed in the ground, there is continuity between what you put in the ground and what comes up. A barley seed produces barley. An acorn becomes an oak tree. A grain of wheat produces wheat. But there is also vast change. Think of the difference between an acorn and a mighty oak. Or the difference between a brown, ugly, hairy tulip bulb and the beautiful flower. You can't imagine the grandeur and majesty of a mighty oak by looking at an acorn. That's the way it will be with our new body. There is continuity between the body (seed) that is buried (planted), but also incredible change that we can't imagine by looking at our earthly bodies.

To use another illustration from nature, the change will be as dramatic as the ugly caterpillar that transforms into a beautiful butterfly. The magnificent winged creature is the same being as the fuzzy insect, yet vastly different.

Paul gives us the best word about our new body in 1 Corinthians 15:43, where he tells us that our new body will be full of glory and will never disappoint us. In this life there is some part of everyone's body (or maybe several parts) that he or she would like to change. In 2003, Americans spent $8.4 billion on nearly 3 million cosmetic plastic surgeries and procedures.[68] Liposuction rates were four times higher in 2003 than in 1992. Botox injections, costing an average of $376 each, more than doubled from 2001 to 2003.

What part of your appearance would you alter if you could? Maybe it's your weight, your height, your hair, your shape, your facial features, or whatever. Our culture accentuates these imperfections by focusing so much attention on physical appearance. We are bombarded daily by ideal images of beautiful, well-built people. But in heaven, there will be no fad diets, no Weight Watchers, no aerobics, no exercise bikes, no personal trainers, no physical therapists, no stair-climbers, no weight rooms, no saunas, no jogging tracks, no low-fat foods, no diet drinks, and no plastic surgeons. God will give every one of His children a glorious, unique, diverse, perfect, glorious new body at the Rapture that will never disappoint.

But in the meantime, before you get your new body, here are a few pointers for living in the body you have now.

1. Thank God for the body you have now. God designed it too, so accept it.
2. Don't compare your body to others. God planned the distinctions among us.
3. Take care of your body as a temple of God's Holy Spirit.
4. Acknowledge the limitations you face.
5. Look forward to the future body God has prepared for you.

Chapter 48

WHEN DO WE GET OUR NEW BODY?

The Bible is clear that every believer in Christ will receive a new body fit for God's eternal kingdom. And it gives us a small glimpse of what these bodies will be like. But when do we get them?

The answer? At the Rapture. When Jesus comes back to rapture His bride, the church, to heaven, every church-age believer will get a new body. The bodies of believers who have died will be raised first, incorruptible and imperishable. At that time these perfected bodies will be rejoined to their perfected spirits that have been with the Lord since the time of their death. Then, those who are alive on earth at the time of the Rapture will undergo an immediate, instantaneous transformation as they are "caught up," or raptured, to heaven. This transformation will occur in less time than it takes to blink your eye.

This resurrection of the dead and translation of the living is described in two main places in the New Testament.

First Corinthians 15:50–53 says:

Now I say this, brethren, that flesh and blood cannot inherit the kingdom of God; nor does the perishable inherit the imperishable. Behold, I tell you a mystery; we will not all sleep, but we will all be changed, in a moment, in the twinkling of an eye, at the last trumpet; for the trumpet will sound, and the dead will be raised imperishable, and we will be changed. For this perishable must put on the imperishable, and this mortal must put on immortality.

A parallel passage, 1 Thessalonians 4:15–17, declares:

For this we say to you by the word of the Lord, that we who are alive and remain until the coming of the Lord, will not precede those who have fallen asleep. For the Lord Himself will descend from heaven with a shout, with the voice of the archangel and with the trumpet of God, and the dead in Christ will rise first. Then we who are alive and remain will be caught up together with them in the clouds to meet the Lord in the air, and so we shall always be with the Lord.

My prayer is that Jesus will come in my lifetime so I can do an end-run on the grave. As one of my friends used to say, "I'm looking for the uppertaker, not the undertaker."

But either way, and whenever the Rapture comes, God will give each of us a brand-new body.

Chapter 49

DO PEOPLE IN HEAVEN RIGHT NOW HAVE A TEMPORARY BODY?

Since those who have died don't get their eternal resurrection body until the Rapture, many people believe that in the meantime God gives His people a temporary body.

The main support for a temporary body comes from four principal passages. The first one is 2 Corinthians 5:1–4:

> For we know that if the earthly tent which is our house is torn down, we have a building from God, a house not made with hands, eternal in the heavens. For indeed in this house we groan, longing to be clothed with our dwelling from heaven, inasmuch as we, having put it on, will not be found naked. For indeed while we are in this tent, we groan, being burdened, because we do not want

to be unclothed but to be clothed, so that what is mortal may be swallowed up by life.

This passage indicates that man, in relation to his body, can be found in one of three conditions.

1. *"Clothed"*: This refers to life in our present earthly body, which is likened to a suit of clothes. Our spirit is clothed in a body.
2. *"Unclothed" or "Naked"*: This refers to life in heaven in the intermediate state when the believer is without a body.
3. *"Clothed"* (literally "clothed upon" in the last part of verse 4): Like putting an overcoat over the clothes you already have on, this makes reference to those who live until the Rapture, and put their new glorified body on right over on top of their present mortal body. Paul said this was his preferred choice of the three. I say "amen" to that!

It seems to me that 2 Corinthians 5 must refer to the final resurrection body each believer receives, not a temporary body, because the body is called "eternal in the heavens" at the end of verse 1. If it's eternal, then it can't be temporary. Second Corinthians 5:1–4 teaches that we will be "naked" or bodiless during the intermediate state in the time before we receive our eternal body.

A second argument for "temporary, intermediate bodies" may be drawn from Luke 16:19–31. It appears that both the rich man and Lazarus have bodies immediately after they die. The rich man refers to Lazarus dipping his finger in some water and placing it on his burning tongue. While this could be used to teach the existence of temporary bodies, we need to be careful, since the point of this passage is not to teach about bodies in heaven and hell, but rather about the torment of the rich man in hell.

Third, at the Transfiguration of Jesus in Matthew 17:1–3, Moses and Elijah appeared with Jesus in bodily form. So, it seems they had some kind of temporary bodily existence. It's likely, however, that in this special instance that God gave Moses and Elijah bodies so they could appear to the disciples visibly with Jesus. All their appearance proves for sure is that they had a body for this one unique event in the life of Jesus. It doesn't prove that all believers have temporary bodies for the full duration of the intermediate state.

Fourth, in Revelation 6:11 a group of martrys in heaven before the resurrection are described as wearing white robes. Many point to this for support of the idea of a temporary body, since disembodied spirits don't wear clothes. However, Revelation 6:9, referring to these same martyrs, says that the apostle John saw the "souls of those who had been slain because of the word of God." Notice he only saw their souls, not their bodies. Therefore, to avoid a contradiction between these two verses, it's probably best in this context to see the white robes not as actual, physical clothing, but as symbolic of Christ's righteousness.

Another important argument against the idea of a temporary body is that between His death and resurrection Jesus was a disembodied spirit (1 Peter 3:18–19). Since this was true of Jesus it only makes sense that it will be true of us as well.

For these reasons (though I can't be hard-and-fast on the issue), it appears to me that during the interval between one's death and the future resurrection of the eternal body at the Rapture, there is no temporary body. Believers in heaven right now exist in a bodiless state.

They, like us, eagerly await the redemption of their bodies (Romans 8:23).

Chapter 50

HOW OLD WILL
WE APPEAR TO BE
IN HEAVEN?

The Bible never explicitly tells us how old we will be or appear to be on the other side. Answering this question, then, requires a bit of sanctified speculation.

We know that God created Adam and Eve with apparent age, that is, they were not created as children who went through the normal stages of physical development. Presumably, Adam and Eve were created at the optimal stage of physical development, for God declared that they were "very good" (Genesis 1:31). Also, when Jesus died, He was resurrected at the prime of His physical development. Jesus was at least thirty-five years old when He died—and possibly as old as thirty-seven or thirty-eight. When He was resurrected He came back in a body recognizable by His followers, so it must have appeared to be about the same age as when He died.

The Roman Catholic theologian Thomas Aquinas (1225–1274) speculated quite a bit about the nature of our future resurrection body. Based on Ephesians 4:13, he maintained that since Jesus was in the stature of the fullness of His physical humanity at age thirty, that our resurrection body will be like the one we had at that age.[69]

The Bible says that when we receive our new resurrection bodies they will be like Jesus' resurrection body (Philippians 3:20–21). While this doesn't necessarily mean that our body will appear how we looked (or will look) in our thirties, it does mean that our body will be perfect. There will be absolutely no blemishes or deformities.

What we can safely say is that the Lord will give us a body that reflects how we looked in the prime of our earthly life. For those who died before they reached the prime of life, the Lord who knows all things will give them a body that reflects how they would have appeared at the optimal stage of development in their life.

PART EIGHT

The Residents of Heaven

Chapter 51

DO PEOPLE WHO COMMIT SUICIDE GO TO HEAVEN?

Suicide is a growing problem in our society. In North America, suicide is the third leading cause of death for people fifteen to twenty-five years of age. Amazingly, among children five to fourteen years of age, suicide is the sixth most common cause of death. Someone commits suicide in America every seventeen minutes.

Whenever someone commits suicide, people often wonder if that person can go to heaven. I have been asked this questions many, many times. Most people seem to think that suicide cannot be forgiven, because the person who died cannot repent of the act or ask for forgiveness. When you really think about it, however, this is true of many sins that all of us commit. Certainly every believer will die with sins that he or she did not even know about and repent of.

There are seven accounts of suicide in the Bible.

1. Abimelech (Judges 9:50–54).
2. Samson (Judges 16:23–31).
3. Saul (1 Samuel 31:2–4).
4. Saul's Servant (1 Samuel 31:5).
5. Ahithophel (2 Samuel 17:23).
6. Zimri (1 Kings 16:15–20).
7. Judas (Matthew 27:3–5).

The Bible, of course, never condones taking one's life. God affirms life. We are creatures made in His image and likeness. Human life is precious. God's command not to murder applies to oneself as well as others.

But we must also say that in none of these cases does the Bible ever state that the person was condemned to hell for committing suicide. In fact, we know that Samson, who took his own life, was a believer; his name appears in the New Testament in the great hall of faith in Hebrews 11:32–34.

People sometimes appeal to 1 Corinthians 3:16–17 as a proof text that people who commit suicide will be excluded from heaven. It says, "Do you not know that you are a temple of God and that the Spirit of God dwells in you? If any man destroys the temple of God, God will destroy him, for the temple of God is holy, and that is what you are." It is important in these verses to notice that the word *you* is not singular, but plural. The individual believer in Christ is a temple of the Holy Spirit according to 1 Corinthians 6:19. But here in 1 Corinthians 3:16–17, Paul refers to the whole community of believers at Corinth. The apostle declares that if anyone destroys the local church, the temple of God, then God will bring severe discipline on that person.

Gordon Fee, a well-known New Testament scholar, agrees with this interpretation:

> Most likely Paul meant by this not that the Spirit dwelt in each of them, true as that would be for him (cf. 6:19), but that the Spirit of God "lives in your midst." That is, Paul is here reflecting on the church as the corporate place of God's dwelling, who, when gathered in Jesus' name, experienced the presence and power of the Lord Jesus in their midst.[70]

For this reason, I believe Paul's words in 1 Corinthians 3:16–17 have nothing to do with the issue of suicide.

There are several cases in the Bible of God's people becoming so discouraged that they wanted to die. Elijah and Jonah are two examples (1 Kings 19:4; Jonah 4:8). I like what Ron Rhodes says about this:

> But these individuals did not take matters into their own hands and kill themselves. Instead they let God rescue them. We can learn a lesson here. When we are filled with despair, we must turn to God and not commit suicide. God will see us through…we too must depend on God when life gets rough.[71]

Nevertheless, while we may not like to admit it, even a true believer can become so troubled, depressed, or even mentally ill that he or she might seek to "end it all." We probably all know someone we consider to be a believer in Christ who took this tragic step. I believe the Bible teaches that the Lord will welcome home any person who has trusted Him, regardless of what he or she has done.

The great comfort that we have as God's children is that nothing can separate us from the love of God in Christ Jesus. The biblical support for this comforting position is Romans 8:38–39: "For I am convinced that neither death, nor life, nor angels, nor principalities, nor things present, nor things to come, nor powers, nor height, nor depth , nor any other created thing, will be able to separate us from the love of God, which is in Christ Jesus our Lord."

Those who have fled to Christ for refuge can never be lost. *No matter what!*

Praise God for His unending, eternal love for us that will never let us go, no matter how seriously or tragically we may fail. His grace always goes beyond our sin. "But where sin increased, grace abounded all the more" (Romans 5:20).

Chapter 52

CAN HOMOSEXUALS GO TO HEAVEN?

Homosexuality has quickly become one of the key moral, social, and political issues of our time. This behavior, which only recently was almost universally condemned as sinful, has now become accepted to the point that the issue of "gay marriage" is front and center in the cultural debate. Mainline denominations struggle with whether homosexuality is sinful—and whether practicing homosexuals can serve as pastors, priests, or bishops. There are even many churches that specifically cater to homosexuals.

But what does the Bible say? Is this lifestyle acceptable to God? Is it equal in His sight to heterosexuality? Can those who practice it go to heaven?

First, the Bible is clear in both the Old and New Testaments that the practice of homosexuality is sinful. There *is* no way around it.

You shall not lie with a male as one lies with a female; it is an abomination. (Leviticus 18:22)

If there is a man who lies with a male as those who lie with a woman, both of them have committed a detestable act; they shall surely be put to death. Their bloodguiltiness is upon them. (Leviticus 20:13)

For this reason God gave them over to degrading passions; for their women exchanged the natural function for that which is unnatural, and in the same way also the men abandoned the natural function of the woman and burned in their desire toward one another, men with men committing indecent acts and receiving in their own persons the due penalty of their error. And just as they did not see fit to acknowledge God any longer, God gave them over to a depraved mind, to do those things which are not proper. (Romans 1:26–28)

…realizing the fact that law is not made for a righteous person, but for those who are lawless and rebellious, for the ungodly and sinners, for the unholy and profane, for those who kill their fathers or mothers, for murderers and immoral men and homosexuals and kidnappers and liars and perjurers, and whatever else is contrary to sound teaching. (1 Timothy 1:9–10)

Second, let me make it clear that God loves homosexuals. God loves all sinners. There is no sin so bad that it cuts one off from the saving grace of God in Christ Jesus. Any sinner who admits his or her sinfulness before God, acknowledges who Jesus is and what He has done, and accepts Him as Savior and Lord by faith is forgiven by God. His blood cleanses us from all sin.

Third, while God loves all sinners and offers them salvation by His grace through faith in Jesus Christ, those who persist in an unrepentant, sinful lifestyle demonstrate that they really don't have a relationship with God through Jesus Christ. This is crystal clear in 1 Corinthians 6:9–11:

> Or do you not know that the unrighteous will not inherit the kingdom of God? Do not be deceived; neither fornicators, nor idolaters, nor adulterers, nor effeminate, nor homosexuals, nor thieves, nor the covetous, nor drunkards, nor revilers, nor swindlers, will inherit the kingdom of God. Such were some of you; but you were washed, but you were sanctified, but you were justified in the name of the Lord Jesus Christ and in the Spirit of our God.

Notice two important things about these verses. First, homosexuality is not singled out. It's just one of many sinful lifestyles that God condemns. Second, those in Corinth who had genuinely accepted God's righteousness in Christ no longer practiced these lifestyles. In 1 Corinthians 6:11 Paul says, "Such *were* some of you." It was in their past.

Did any of the Corinthians continue to struggle with sin in their lives? Sure they did. Just read the entire letter of 1 Corinthians. But they no longer sinned with impunity. They no longer lived this way as their continual practice of life.

What this passage tells us is that how we live shows what we really are. Regardless of one's religious profession, or what one says, a person whose life is habitually marked by any of these catalogued sins is not saved (see 1 John 3:6–10). Twice in these verses God affirms that people who live these sinful lifestyles "shall not inherit the kingdom of God."

What should we conclude, then? That anyone who claims to be a true believer in Christ and says that he or she is going to heaven and yet at the same time lives the homosexual lifestyle is flatly contradicting what God says in 1 Corinthians 6:9–11.

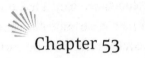

Chapter 53

WILL THERE BE ANIMALS IN HEAVEN?

You might be surprised how frequently people ask this question.

Not long ago I was reading Billy Graham's Q & A column in our local paper, and a man asked if his pet would be in heaven with him and his family.

In my own ministry, I've been asked that same question time and again—by people of all ages. In fact, it probably rates up at the top of the most-asked questions about life after death.

And you have to be careful how you answer! This issue stirs up a great deal of emotion for those who deeply love their pets. In a monthly magazine I receive, the editor answered a question that had been sent in about animals in heaven.[72] The next month he received a passionate response from people taking the other side of the issue. The editor closed his answer to the comments with this statement: "Incidentally, the issue of animals in heaven has generated more responses than any other subject."[73]

Certainly seeing our pets in heaven should not be our focus. Our blessed Savior will be the main, all-consuming focus of heaven. The Lamb of God will draw our attention and adoration more than anything or anyone else. At the same time, however, our focus on Jesus will in no way detract from our enjoyment of one another and the beauty of the heavenly paradise. And part of this beauty and enjoyment may include our pets from here on earth.

Those who don't believe there will be animals in heaven often point to Genesis 2:7, which says, "Then the LORD God formed man of dust from the ground, and breathed into his nostrils the breath of life; and man became a living being." This verse is theological fuel for those who maintain that only man and woman have souls. The Bible never says that God breathed life into animals.

Does that settle the issue, then?

Not in my book.

Although all would agree that Scripture does not say conclusively whether our pets will be in heaven, three key points lead me to believe that animals in general—and pets in particular—will be with us on the other side.

First, animals were part of the original creation of God that was declared "good." The Garden of Eden, called Paradise, was filled with animals (Genesis 1:25). Revelation tells us that heaven will contain many of the same things that were in the original creation, such as a river, trees, and fruit. Why not animals too? After all, animals are an integral part of earthly life, and testify powerfully of the creative, imaginative genius of God. He created the giraffe, the camel, the platypus, the lion, the pachyderm, and the hummingbird. As W. A. Criswell notes, "God has shown a penchant for varieties of life-forms, and it would be difficult to imagine that this would not be perpetuated in the heavenlies."[74]

Concerning the question of animals in general in heaven,

Peter Kreeft says, "The simplest answer is: Why not? How irrational is the prejudice that would allow plants (green fields and flowers) but not animals in heaven!"[75]

Concerning the more difficult issue of whether the same animals will be in heaven that were here on earth, Kreeft adds:

> Would the same animals be in heaven as on earth? "Is my dead cat in heaven?" Again, why not? God can raise up the very grass; why not cats? Though the blessed have better things to do than play with pets, the better does not exclude the lesser. We were meant from the beginning to have stewardship over the animals; we have not fulfilled that divine plan yet on earth; therefore it seems likely that the right relationship with animals will be part of Heaven; proper "petship." And what better place to begin than with the already petted pets?[76]

C. S. Lewis maintained that animals belonging to believers are saved in and through their masters as a kind of part of their extended family.[77]

Second, the Bible affirms from beginning to end that animals have souls. In Genesis 1:20, 24 we find the Hebrew word for *soul (nepes)* used of animals. This word refers to the passionate appetites and desires of all living things, including the drives for sex and food.[78] Also, Revelation 8:9 uses the Greek word for *soul (psuchas)* in reference to sea creatures—although this word can sometimes have the meaning of "physical life."

Of course, the soul of an animal is qualitatively very different from the soul of a human being. The human soul craves God as well as sex and food. But the fact that animals have souls may indicate that all or some of them will be resurrected in the afterlife.

Third, in the millennial kingdom, or thousand-year reign of

Christ on earth, animals will be present in abundance. Isaiah 11:6–8 paints the picture of animal life in the kingdom.

> And the wolf will dwell with the lamb, and the leopard will lie down with the young goat, and the calf and the young lion and the fatling together; and a little boy will lead them. Also the cow and the bear will graze, their young will lie down together, and the lion will eat straw like the ox. The nursing child will play by the hole of the cobra, and the weaned child will put his hand on the viper's den.

While the thousand-year reign of Christ is not heaven or the eternal state, it is the initial phase or "front porch" of the eternal kingdom of God. Therefore, since animals exist in the millennium, this at least establishes a precedent for suggesting that animals will populate the eternal state or new earth that God will create (Revelation 21:1).

In her book *Holiness in Hidden Places,* Joni Eareckson Tada talks about whether she will see her pet schnauzer, Scrappy, in heaven. Her words are a poignant summary of this issue.

> If God brings our pets back to life, it wouldn't surprise me. It would be just like Him. It would be totally in keeping with His generous character.... Exorbitant. Excessive. Extravagant in grace after grace. Of all the dazzling discoveries and ecstatic pleasures heaven will hold for us, the potential of seeing Scrappy would be pure whimsy—utterly, joyfully, surprisingly superfluous.... Heaven is going to be a place that will refract and reflect in as many ways as possible the goodness and joy of our great God, who delights in lavishing love on His children. So will pets be in heaven? Who knows?[79]

Chapter 54

DO INFANTS AND CHILDREN WHO DIE GO TO HEAVEN?

O ne of the most horrible experiences a person can face in this life is the loss of a small child. We all know families that have suffered this tragic trauma. When this occurs, the parents—especially if they are believers in Christ—want to know if they will see their child again someday in heaven.

There are two main views on this important topic.

View #1: Yes and no.
Those who hold to this position say that some children who die will go heaven, and others will not. There are variations in how this is explained. Some say that children who are elect go to heaven while the non-elect don't—and only God knows which is which. The *Westminster Confession* (ch. X) states, "Elect infants, dying in infancy, are regenerated and saved by Christ through the Spirit, who works when and where and how he pleases."

Others say that God, in His omniscience, or ability to know everything, looked down the corridors of time and saw hypothetically which children would have believed had they lived to maturity and that these children are brought to heaven when they die.

View #2: Yes, always.

Those who hold to this position insist that all who die without the ability to understand or believe the truth of the gospel go to heaven. This would include pre-born children, infants, young children, and those who suffer from serious mental challenges.

This is the view that I believe best represents the teaching of the Bible. But how does this work? How can God let people into heaven who have not believed in His Son?

THE "AGE OF ACCOUNTABILITY"

One crucial Bible teaching we must recognize is that—with the exception of the mentally handicapped—every person does reach a time of personal, moral accountability before the Creator. Every human being born on this planet reaches the point when he or she becomes personally responsible for accepting or rejecting Jesus Christ. This point in time has most often been referred to as the "age of accountability." You won't find these exact words in the Bible. It's simply a phrase theologians have developed to express the biblical concept.

One of my friends who lives in Texas asked me recently if I knew why all Texas Aggies will go to heaven. When I told him that I didn't, he responded, "Because none of them ever reach the age of accountability." (It's just a joke!)

Most Christians have probably heard of the idea of an "age of accountability" at some time in their life. It's a common way to understand and explain what happens to children or the mentally handicapped when they die.

The issue here is that small children and those with serious mental challenges cannot do the one thing that is required to enter heaven—believe in Jesus Christ as Savior from sin. Nor can they consciously do the one thing that condemns a person to hell—reject the gospel of Jesus Christ. They can't do this for the simple reason that they can't understand it. I believe this also includes pre-born children as well whose lives are terminated by miscarriage or abortion, since I believe the Bible teaches that human life begins at conception.

So what happens to those who are unable to meet the one biblical condition for salvation? Even though they are small, helpless, and beautiful, they still possess the stain of original sin (Psalm 51:5). They are born in sin. What's the solution? It seems to me that God applies the benefits of Christ's saving death and resurrection to the person at the moment of death. At that moment the person is saved, and is immediately brought into God's presence in heaven.[80]

People sometimes ask the question, "Does this mean then that all these children and babies are part of God's elect?" My answer to that is yes. I believe this is what the Bible says.

But I don't want you to take my word for it.

Let's see if the Bible supports this idea.

The Testimony of King David

King David, after the loss of his child with Bathsheba, said these heart-wrenching words:

> "While the child was still alive, I fasted and wept; for I said, 'Who knows, the LORD may be gracious to me, that the child may live.' But now he has died; why should I fast? Can I bring him back again? I will go to him, but he will not return to me." (2 Samuel 12:22–23)

Some believe that all David meant by these words is that someday he too would die. But why would David need to say this? Everyone knew he would die. That was obvious. It makes more sense to draw this conclusion: David was saying that while his child could not return to earth, David would go to be with him in heaven—indicating his belief that his child was in heaven.

THE TESTIMONY OF JESUS

Nearly a thousand years later, during His earthly ministry, Jesus too seemed to indicate that children are part of God's kingdom.

> And He called a child to Himself and set him before them, and said, "Truly I say to you, unless you are converted and become like children, you will not enter the kingdom of heaven." (Matthew 18:2–3)

> But Jesus said, "Let the children alone, and do not hinder them from coming to Me; for the kingdom of heaven belongs to such as these." (Matthew 19:14)

That's why we sing the simple yet profound words, "Jesus loves the little children…they are precious in His sight."

SCRIPTURAL SILENCE

Another point that should be considered is that in addition to the positive testimony from the lips of David and Jesus, there is a deafening biblical silence concerning any infants or children in hell. While one must always be careful with arguments from silence, the silence on this issue is worth noting. Robert Lightner, a professor of systematic theology, says, "Not once in all the references to infants is there so much as a hint that they will ever be damned to eternal perdition after death, should they die before they have opportunity to respond to the gospel."[81]

WILL THEY REMAIN AS CHILDREN?

One other related question always comes up when discussing this topic. Will these babies and small children remain in that state when they get to heaven? I have heard some preachers and teachers speculate that they may remain as babies until the thousand-year reign of Christ on the earth, at which time God will arrange for them to be raised by their saved parents during earth's golden age. While this is a comforting thought for many parents, there is no biblical evidence that this is true.

CONCLUSION

When it comes to the issue of salvation for children or those with serious mental challenges, there are at least three significant points we should keep in mind.

One...at some point, every person who grows to maturity, except those with serious mental challenges, reaches a point of personal, moral accountability before God to either accept or reject the gospel of Jesus Christ.

Two...if a child dies before reaching this age of accountability, or if due to mental challenges a person never reaches this point, the Lord applies the saving benefits of Christ's redeeming work to that person at the moment of death and brings that soul immediately into His presence in heaven.

Three...this saving grace of God would also embrace pre-born children—those whose lives are terminated by miscarriage or abortion.

PART NINE

Life's
Greatest
Question

Chapter 55

WILL YOU GO
TO HEAVEN?

Having done my best to answer fifty-four questions about life after death from a biblical perspective, I've saved this question for last.

It's your turn.

The question is very simple, yet it's the most profound and weighty question you will ever answer in all your days: Will you go to heaven either when the Lord comes or when you die? Are you prepared? Are you ready?

Is heaven in your future?

It's imperative that you face this question right now. It has powerful implications both for this life and the next.

For this life, it will allow you to really live. I've heard it said many times that "only those who are prepared to die are really prepared to live." It's true. Only people who know for sure that they have eternal life can live this life to the fullest.

And for the next life, the stakes could not be higher. It's been well said that for believers in Christ, this life is the only hell we will ever know. But for unbelievers, this life is the only heaven they will ever know. So the importance of acting now cannot be exaggerated. No one knows how much time he or she has *personally*—any one of us could die with the next heartbeat, the next breath. And death will end any chance for you to reconsider or change your mind. At the same time, not one of us knows how much time we have *prophetically*—Jesus could come today.

So, how can you know for sure that you will go to heaven?

The answer to this question depends on one simple issue: What have you done with Jesus?

If you're still not sure if heaven's in your future, let me share a few very simple thoughts with you.

GOD'S PLAN OF SALVATION

God's Word declares that all men and women are sinners, both by nature and by action (Romans 3:23). The Bible also declares that God is infinitely holy, righteous, and just and cannot accept sinners into His holy presence. As you can see right off, this is a major problem. How can a holy God accept sinful human beings?

Lewis Sperry Chafer, the founder of Dallas Seminary, once said that any person can come up with a plan by which good people can go to heaven, but only God can devise a plan by which a sinner, who is His enemy, can go to heaven.[82]

God, in His infinite wisdom and grace, formulated a plan to remedy this problem. God the Son agreed to step out of eternity into time, to take on human flesh, to live the sinless life we can never live, and to die as a substitute for sinful humanity. He took all our sins on Himself and paid the eternal price for our sins, bearing the full wrath of the Father for us on the cross. Just before He died, Jesus cried out, "It is finished."

The Father then raised the Son from the dead three days

later to prove that He had accepted the full payment for our sins. Because of this finished work of Christ, it is now possible for sinful men and women to have a relationship with a holy God. A full provision for sin has been made. "The LORD has caused the iniquity of us all to fall on Him" (Isaiah 53:6).

YOUR RESPONSE

God's solution to the sin problem is clear. All that remains for any person to have a relationship with a holy God forever is for that person to recognize his need for salvation, to realize that he cannot do anything to earn or merit this salvation, and to personally receive by faith the full provision God has made. Carefully read these words from Scripture and ask God to make them clear in your heart and mind.

But as many as received Him, to them He gave the right to become the children of God, even to those who believe in His name. (John 1:12)

For the wages of sin is death, but the free gift of God is eternal life in Christ Jesus our Lord. (Romans 6:23).

For by grace you have been saved through faith; and that not of yourselves, it is the gift of God; not as a result of works, so that no one may boast. (Ephesians 2:8–9)

Why not remove all doubt about where you will spend eternity?

God is offering you the free gift of eternal life. Don't wait. Receive the Savior now. Receive the gift. Call upon Jesus right now in prayer and He will save you. God's Word says that "whoever will call on the name of the Lord will be saved" (Romans 10:13).

It is the greatest decision you will ever make. When you trust Christ, you will immediately have a place reserved for you in heaven (1 Peter 1:4). You can be sure from this time on that you *will* go to heaven, either at the Rapture when Christ comes or when your time on earth is up and your soul slips into eternity.

Why not call upon the Lord right now to receive His gracious pardon by praying a simple prayer like the one below? There are no magic words that will bring salvation. God looks at the heart. But if this prayer expresses the sincere desire of your heart to receive Christ as your personal Savior, God will save you right now. However and wherever you may be.

> *Father, I come to You now and admit that I'm a sinner. And I know that I need a Savior. I acknowledge that I can never earn my own way to heaven. I accept Jesus as the Savior I need. I believe that He died on the cross and rose again for me. I call upon You to save me. Thank You for saving me and allowing me to know You personally. Amen.*

THE FATHER'S SON

Years ago, there was a very wealthy man who, with his devoted young son, shared a passion for art collecting. Together they traveled around the world, adding only the finest art treasures to their collection. Priceless works by Picasso, van Gogh, Monet, and many others adorned the walls of the family estate. The widowed elder man looked on with satisfaction as his only child became an experienced art collector. The son's trained eye and sharp business mind caused his father to beam with pride as they dealt with art collectors around the world.

As winter approached, war engulfed the nation, and the young man left to serve his country. After only a few short weeks, his father received a telegram. His beloved son was missing in action. The art collector anxiously awaited more news, fearing he would never see his son again. Within days, his fears were confirmed. The young man had died while rushing a fellow soldier to a medic. Distraught and lonely, the old man faced the upcoming Christmas holidays with anguish and sadness. The joy of the season, a season that he and his son had so looked forward to, would visit his house no longer.

On Christmas morning, a knock on the door awakened the depressed old man. As he walked to the door, the masterpieces of art on the walls only reminded him that his son was not coming home. Opening the door, he was greeted by a soldier with a large package in his hand. He introduced himself to the man by saying, "I was a friend of your son. I was the one he was rescuing when he died. May I come in for a few moments? I have something to show you."

As the two began to talk, the soldier told of how the man's son had told everyone of his, not to mention his father's, love of fine art. "I'm something of an artist myself," said the soldier, "and I want to give you this." As the old man unwrapped the package, the paper gave way to reveal a portrait of the man's son. Though the world would never consider it a work of a genius, the painting featured the young man's face in striking detail.

Overcome with emotion, the man thanked the soldier, promising to hang the picture above the fireplace. A few hours later, after the soldier had departed, the old man set about his task. True to his word, the painting went above the fireplace, pushing aside thousands of dollars of paintings. Then the man sat in his chair and spent Christmas gazing at the gift he had been given.

During the days and weeks that followed, the man realized that even though his son was no longer with him, the boy's life would live on because of those he had touched. He would soon learn that his son had rescued dozens of wounded soldiers before a bullet stilled his caring heart. As the stories of his son's gallantry continued to reach him, fatherly pride and satisfaction began to ease the grief. The painting of his son soon became his most prized possession, far eclipsing any interest in the pieces for which museums around the world clamored. He told his neighbors it was the greatest gift he had ever received.

The following spring, the old man became ill and passed away. The art world was in anticipation! Unmindful of the story of the man's only son—but in his honor—those paintings would be sold at an auction.

According to the will of the old man, all of the art works would be auctioned on Christmas day, the day he had received his greatest gift. The day soon arrived, and art collectors from around the world gathered to bid on some of the world's most spectacular paintings. Dreams would be fulfilled this day; greatness would be achieved as many would claim "I have the greatest collection."

The auction began with a painting that was not on any museum's list. It was the painting of the man's son. The auctioneer asked for an opening bid. The room was silent. "Who will open the bidding with $100?" he asked. Minutes passed. No one spoke. From the back of the room came, "Who cares about that painting? It's just a picture of his son. Let's forget it and go on to the good stuff." More voices echoed in agreement.

"No," replied the auctioneer, "we have to sell this one first. Now, who will take the son?"

Finally, a friend of the old man spoke. "Will you take ten dollars for the painting? That's all I have. I knew the boy, so I'd like to have it."

"I have ten dollars," called the auctioneer. "Will anyone go higher?" After more silence, the auctioneer said, "Going once, going twice. Gone."

The gavel fell. Cheers filled the room and someone exclaimed, "Now we can get on with it and bid on these treasures!" The auctioneer looked at the audience and announced that the auction was over.

Stunned disbelief quieted the room. Someone spoke up and asked, "What do you mean, it's over? We didn't come here for a picture of some old guy's son. What about all of these paintings? There are millions of dollars' worth of art here! I demand that you explain what's going on here!"

The auctioneer replied, "It's very simple. According to the will of the father, whoever takes the son...gets it all."[83]

What a great truth for us to contemplate. If we have the Son, we get it all. The total inheritance. As we have seen, our inheritance both in this life and the life to come is unimaginable.

Make sure your eternal inheritance is secure.

Make sure you "take the Son"!

Recommended Books
for Further Study

Bayly, Joseph. *The View from a Hearse: A Christian View of Death.* Elgin, IL: David C. Cook Publishing Co., 1969.

Benware, Paul N. *The Believer's Payday.* Chattanooga, TN: AMG Publishers, 2002.

Blanchard, John. *Whatever Happened to Hell?* Durham, England: Evangelical Press, 1993.

Boettner, Loraine. *Immortality.* Philipsburg, NJ: The Presbyterian and Reformed Publishing Co., 1956.

Criswell, W. A. and Paige Patterson. *Heaven.* Wheaton, IL: Tyndale House Publishers, 1991.

Crockett, William, gen. ed. *Four Views on Hell.* Counterpoints. Series Editor Stanley N. Gundry. Grand Rapids. MI: Zondervan Publishing House, 1996.

Dixon, Larry. *Heaven: Thinking Now About Forever.* Camp Hill, PA: Christian Publications, Inc., 2002.

———. *The Other Side of the Good News.* Wheaton, IL: Bridgepoint, 1992.

Eareckson Tada, Joni. *Heaven, Your Real Home.* Grand Rapids, MI: Zondervan Publishing House, 1995.

Evans, Tony. *Tony Evans Speaks Out on Heaven and Hell.* Chicago, IL: Moody Press, 2000.

Graham, Billy. *Death and the Life After.* Nashville, TN: W Publishing Group, 1987.

Habermas, Gary R., and J. P. Moreland. *Immortality: The Other Side of Death.* Nashville, TN: Thomas Nelson Publishers, 1992.

Hanegraaff, Hank. *Resurrection.* Nashville, TN: Word Publishing, 2000.

Hendriksen, William. *The Bible on the Life Hereafter.* Grand Rapids, MI: Baker Book House, 1959.

Ice, Thomas, and Timothy Demy. *The Truth About Heaven and Eternity*. Eugene, OR: Harvest House Publishers, 1997.

Kreeft, Peter. *Everything You Ever Wanted to Know About Heaven, but Never Dreamed of Asking!* San Francisco, CA: Ignatius Press, 1990.

LaHaye, Tim. *Life in the Afterlife*. Wheaton, IL: Tyndale House Publishers, 1980.

Lawson, Steven J. *Heaven Help Us!* Colorado Springs, CO: NavPress, 1995.

Lightner, Robert. *Heaven for Those Who Can't Believe*. Schaumberg, IL: Regular Baptist Press, 1977.

Lotz, Anne Graham. *Heaven: My Father's House*. Nashville, TN: W Publishing Group, 2003.

Lloyd, Dan S. *Leading Today's Funerals: A Pastoral Guide for Improving Bereavement Ministry*. Grand Rapids, MI: Baker Books, 1997.

Lutzer, Erwin W. *One Minute After You Die*. Chicago, IL: Moody Press, 1997.

———. *Your Eternal Reward*. Chicago, IL: Moody Press, 1998.

MacArthur, John F. *The Glory of Heaven*. Wheaton, IL: Crossway Books, 1996.

Morey, Robert A. *Death and the Afterlife*. Minneapolis, MN: Bethany House Publishers, 1984.

Rhodes, Ron. *The Undiscovered Country*. Eugene, OR: Harvest House Publishers, 1996.

Rumford, Douglas J. *What about Heaven & Hell?* Wheaton, IL: Tyndale House Publishers, 2000.

Smith, Wilbur. *The Biblical Doctrine of Heaven*. Chicago, IL: Moody Press, 1974.

Wall, Joe L. *Going for the Gold: Reward and Loss at the Judgment Seat of Christ*. Chicago, IL: Moody Press, 1991.

Notes

1. Larry Dixon, *Heaven: Thinking Now About Forever* (Camp Hill, PA: Christian Publications, Inc., 2002), 140.

2. Tony Evans, *Tony Evans Speaks Out on Heaven and Hell* (Chicago, IL: Moody Press, 2000), 7–8.

3. Ron Rhodes, *The Undiscovered Country: Exploring the Wonder of Heaven and the Afterlife* (Eugene, OR: Harvest House Publishers, 1996), 39–40.

4. Evans, *Tony Evans Speaks Out on Heaven and Hell,* 7.

5. Zachary J. Hayes, *Four Views on Hell,* William Crockett, gen. ed. (Grand Rapids, MI:: Zondervan, 1997), 99.

6. Ibid., 93, 98.

7. Cardinal Joseph Ratzinger, *Eschatology: Death and Eternal Life,* trans. A. Nichols (Washington, D.C.: Catholic University of America Press, 1988), 189.

8. Lorraine Boettner, "Purgatory," in *Evangelical Dictionary of Theology,* ed. Walter A. Elwell (Grand Rapids, MI: Baker Book House, 1984), 897.

9. George Hover, *What Happens When I Die?* (Nashville, TN: Abingdon Press, 2004), 15.

10. Rodney Clapp, "Rumors of Heaven," *Christianity Today* (October 7, 1988), 20.

11. Ibid., 25.

12. Billy Graham, *Angels: God's Secret Agents,* rev. ed. (Dallas, TX: Word Publishing, 1986), 114–15.

13. Ibid., 116.

14. Gary R. Habermas and J. P. Moreland. *Immortality: The Other Side of Death* (Nashville: TN: Thomas Nelson Publishers, 1992), 121.

15. *Gallup News Service,* June 8, 2001.

16. Hank Hannegraaf, *Resurrection* (Nashville, TN: Word Publishing, 2000), 125–26.

17. Ibid., 127.
18. *Gallup News Service,* June 8, 2001.
19. *Webster's New Collegiate Dictionary* (Springfield, MA: G & C Merriam Company, 1973), 714.
20. Ibid., 930.
21. Ibid., 768.
22. Michael Gleghorn, "Communicating with the Dead," *Probe Ministries,* 2003. www.probe.org/docs/comm-dead.html (accessed 24 September 2004).
23. Ibid.
24. *World,* 28 July 2001, 22.
25. Evans, *Tony Evans Speaks Out on Heaven and Hell,* 10–11.
26. Taken from Billy Graham, *Approaching Hoofbeats* (Nashville, TN: W Pub Group, 1985), 204.
27. Rhodes, *The Undiscovered Country,* 39–40.
28. Norman L. Geisler and Douglas E. Potter, "From Ashes to Ashes: Is Burial the Only Christian Option?" *Christian Research Journal* (July–September 1998): 29.
29. Hanegraaff, *Resurrection,* 130–31; Timothy George, "Cremation Confusion," *Christianity Today* (May 21, 2002), 66.
30. Douglas J. Rumford, *What About Heaven & Hell?* (Wheaton, IL: Tyndale House Publishers, 2000), 79.
31. Gallup's Tuesday Briefing Report, June 2, 2004.
32. George Barna, "Americans Describe Their Views About Life After Death," *Barna Research Online*, October 21, 2003. http://www.barna.org/FlexPage.aspx?Page=BarnaUpdate&BarnaUpdateID=150 (accessed 27 September 2004).
33. Author unknown.
34. Erwin W. Lutzer, *One Minute After You Die* (Chicago, IL: Moody Press, 1995), 39.
35. William Lane Craig, "The Craig-Bradley Debate: Can a Loving God Send People to Hell?" *The Virtual Office of Dr. William Craig,* 1994. http://www.leaderu.com/offices/billcraig/docs/craig-bradley0.html (accessed 24 September 2004).

36. Ibid.

37. Rich Buhler, "Background on the Drilling to Hell Story," *TruthOrFiction.com.* www.truthorfiction.com/rumors/d/drilltohell-facts.htm (accessed 24 September 2004).

38. William Hendriksen, *Philippians, Colossians and Philemon,* New Testament Commentary (Grand Rapids, MI: Baker Book House, 1979), 115–16.

39. Harold W. Hoehner, *Ephesians* (Grand Rapids, MI: Baker Academic, 2002), 535–36.

40. D. Edmond Hiebert, *1 Peter* (Chicago: Moody Press, 1992), 238–46.

41. Ibid., 266–67.

42. Quoted by Erwin Lutzer, *One Minute After You Die*, 38.

43. Quoted by Larry Dixon, *The Other Side of the Good News* (Wheaton, IL: BridgePoint, 1992), 93.

44. Charles Haddon Spurgeon, "Heaven and Hell," sermons 39, 40, *spurgeongems.org.* http://www.spurgeongems.org/vols1-3/chs39-40.pdf (accessed 27 September 2004).

45. *Time,* 24 March 97, 73.

46. Ibid.

47. Edythe Draper, *Draper's Book of Quotations for the Christian World* (Wheaton, IL: Tyndale House Publishers, 1992), 307.

48. "Why We Need Heaven," *Newsweek,* 12 August 2002, 47.

49. Ray C. Stedman, *God's Final Word: Understanding Revelation* (Grand Rapids, MI: Discovery House, 1991), 333.

50. Steven J. Lawson, *Heaven Help Us!* (Colorado Springs, CO: NavPress, 1995), 158.

51. D. A. Carson, "Matthew," in *The Expositor's Bible Commentary,* gen. ed. Frank E. Gaebelein, vol. 8 (Grand Rapids, MI: Zondervan Publishing House, 1984), 373.

52. Robert L. Thomas, *Revelation 1–7: An Exegetical Commentary* (Chicago: Moody Press, 1992), 396.

53. David Jeremiah, *What the Bible Says About Angels* (Sisters, OR: Multnomah Publishers, 1996), 200.

54. C. Fred Dickason, *Angels, Elect and Evil* (Chicago, IL: Moody Press, 1975), 100.

55. Jeremiah, *What the Bible Says About Angels,* 201.

56. Graham, *Angels: God's Secret Agents,* 116.

57. Ibid.

58. Peter Kreeft, *Everything You Ever Wanted to Know About Heaven, but Never Dreamed of Asking* (San Francisco: Ignatius Press, 1990), 27.

59. Dandi Daley Mackall, *Kids Are Still Saying the Darndest Things* (Rocklin, CA: Prima Publishing, 1994), 26–27.

60. Robert E. Coleman, *Singing with the Angels* (Grand Rapids: Fleming H. Revell, 1980), 53.

61. Kreeft, *Everything You Ever Wanted to Know About Heaven, but Never Dreamed of Asking,* 49–50.

62. Hannegraaf, *Resurrection,* 140–41.

63. Kreeft, *Everything You Ever Wanted to Know About Heaven, but Never Dreamed of Asking,* 131.

64. Robert L. Thomas, *Revelation 8–22* (Chicago: Moody Press, 1995), 484.

65. John MacArthur Jr., *Heaven* (Chicago, IL: Moody Press, 1988), 90.

66. Joni Eareckson Tada, *Heaven: Your Real Home* (Grand Rapids, MI: Zondervan Pubishing Company, 1995), 39.

67. Dr. Harold Willmington, *Eschatology 101: Great Truths from God's Word,* n.d., 262.

68. "A Body of Work," *USA Today,* 29 July 2004, 8D.

69. Rumford, *What About Heaven and Hell,* 24.

70. Gordon D. Fee, *The First Epistle to the Corinthians,* The New International Commentary of the New Testament, gen. ed. F. F. Bruce (Grand Rapids: MI: William B. Eerdmans, 1987), 147.

71. Rhodes, *The Undiscovered Country,* 196.

72. Arno Froese, ed., *The Midnight Call* (September 2003): 42–44.

73. Ibid., (December 2003): 43–44.

74. W. A. Criswell and Paige Patterson, *Heaven* (Wheaton, IL: Tyndale House Publishers, 1991), 53.

75. Kreeft, *Everything You Ever Wanted to Know About Heaven, but Never Dreamed of Asking*, 45.

76. Ibid., 45–46.

77. C. S. Lewis, *The Problem of Pain* (New York: MacMillan, 1962), 138–39.

78. Bruce K. Waltke, *Genesis* (Grand Rapids, MI: Zondervan, 2001), 63.

79. Joni Eareckson Tada, *Holiness in Hidden Places* (Nashville, TN: J. Countryman, 1999), 133.

80. Rhodes, *The Undiscovered Country*, 100–102.

81. Robert Lightner, *Heaven for Those Who Can't Believe* (Schaumburg, IL: Regular Baptist Press, 1977), 18.

82. Criswell and Patterson, *Heaven*, 60.

83. Author unknown.

THE TRUTH BEHIND THE FICTION

The Left Behind books raise powerful and disturbing questions. *Do the authors present an accurate view of end time events? Could we really be that close to those final, terrible years? Do believers dare hope for a rapture that will sweep us into the presence of Christ before God unleashes His righteous judgment on the world?* If these things are true it will certainly change the way we live our lives right now—giving us both a sense of urgency and an enduring hope.

1-59052-366-0

www.endtimesanswers.com

Multnomah® Publishers
Keeping Your Trust…One Book at a Time®

THUNDERING HOOFBEATS

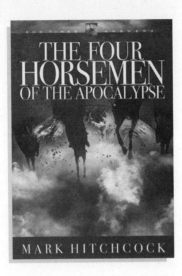

The image of the four horsemen of the Apocalypse in Revelation 6:1–8 is one of the most vivid and powerful in all the writings of the prophets. Their presence speaks of a coming day of horror—the first four judgments of the Tribulation. Events in our world today indicate that they could be mounting up to ride across the earth!

Prophecy expert Mark Hitchcock invites you to take an in-depth look at the four horsemen and provides a *positive word of hope* for your family in the end times.

1-59052-333-4

www.endtimesanswers.com

Multnomah® Publishers
Keeping Your Trust...One Book at a Time®

END TIMES ANSWERS

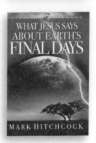